TEACH YOURSELF

English Grammar & Composition

Rajat Chandna

Lotus PRESS

4735/22, Prakash Deep Building
Ansari Road, Darya Ganj,
New Delhi - 110002

Lotus Press : Publishers & Distributors
Unit No. 220, 2nd Floor, 4735/22, Prakash Deep Building,
Ansari Road, Darya Ganj, New Delhi- 110002
Ph.: 23280047, 98118-38000
• E-mail : lotuspress1984@gmail.com
www.lotuspress.co.in

Teach Yourself English Grammar & Composition

ISBN: 978-81-8382-265-7

Printed & Published by : **Lotus Press Publisher & Distributors,** New Delhi-02

TEACH YOURSELF

English Grammar & Composition

Published by :
Lotus Press Publishers & Distributors

PREFACE

The art of speaking and writing clearly and correctly is what every student wants to accomplish. This book is written in the belief that this habit can be attained by most students only through frequent practice in the art of free and spontaneous writing combined with a study of the grammar. In the present book, Grammar and Composition are presented as a systematic study. The special purpose of this study of grammar is to help students make clear sentence structures. In every chapter a careful study of some definite unit of grammar is followed by general examples.

The following are some of its special features:

1. Numerous suggestive lists of composition topics likely to appeal to the varied interests of different types of pupils.
2. Models of good speech. Simple and easy language.
3. The introduction of facts of grammar that would help students choose correctly between inflected forms, construct sentences that 'hang together,' punctuate these sentences correctly, and 'see through' the sentences that they are likely to meet in their reading.
4. Topics are arranged in a manner that one point leads naturally to another. An organised and easily remembered body of facts is developed.

5. Clear and simple statement of definitions and rules.

All of us make mistakes in writing and speaking a language. It is more in the case of English language. These errors may be avoided by us if we are little more careful. A serious study of the book will help the students avoid common pitfalls and speak and write English correctly and confidently.

This book contains basic, rich and essential material on essay writing, letter writing, and story writing as well. The book will act as a guide to the students in the descriptive aspect of writing.

All the sections have been simplified. It will further groom the readers in the basics of the English Language.

Author

CONTENTS

Part I Grammar

Part II Composition

Part I: Grammar

CHAPTER 1

Parts of Speech

On the basis of their grammatical behaviour the words of a language are divided into several classes. These different classes of words are called the parts of speech.

Traditional grammar classifies words based on eight parts of speech: the verb, the noun, the pronoun, the adjective, the adverb, the preposition, the conjunction, and the interjection.

It is important to be able to recognise and identify the different types of words in English, so that you can understand grammar explanations and use the right word form in the right place. Here is a brief explanation of what the parts of speech are:

Noun: A noun is a naming word. It names a person, place, thing, idea, living creature, quality, or action. Example: cowboy, theatre, box, thought, tree, kindness, arrival, etc.

Pronoun: A pronoun is used instead of a noun, to avoid repeating the noun.

Verb: A verb is a word which describes an action (doing

something) or a state (being something). Example: walk, talk, think, believe, live, like, want.

Adverb: An adverb is a word which usually describes a verb. It tells you how something is done. It may also tell you when or where something happened.

Examples: slowly, intelligently, well, yesterday, tomorrow.

Adjective: An adjective is a word that describes a noun. It tells you something about the noun.

Examples: big, yellow, thin, amazing, beautiful, quick, important.

Conjunction: A conjunction joins two words, phrases or sentences together.

Examples: but, so, and, because etc.

Preposition: A preposition usually comes before a noun, pronoun or noun phrase. It joins the noun to some other part of the sentence.

Examples: on, in, by, with, under, through, at etc.

Interjection: An interjection is an unusual kind of word, because it often stands alone. Interjections are words which express emotion or surprise, and they are usually followed by exclamation marks.

Examples: Ouch!, Hello!, Hurray!, Oh no!, Ha!

Parts of Speech Table

This is a summary of the 8 parts of speech.

Part of Speech	Function or 'Job'	Example Words	Example Sentences
Verb	action or state	(to) be, have, do, like, work, sing, can, must	English Club.com is a web site. I like EnglishClub.com.
Noun	thing or person	pen, dog, work, music, town, Mumbai, teacher, Manish	This is my dog. He lives in my house. We live in Mumbai.

Contd..

Adjective	describes a noun	a/an, the, 69, some, good, big, red, well, interesting	My dog is big. I like big dogs.
Adverb	describes a verb, adjective or adverb	quickly, silently, well, badly, very, really	My dog eats quickly. When he is very hungry, he eats really quickly.
Pronoun	replaces a noun	I, you, he, she, some	Tara is Indian. She is beautiful.
Preposition	links a noun to another word	to, at, after, on, but	We went to school on Monday.
Conjunction	joins clauses or sentences or words	and, but, when	I like dogs and I like cats. I like cats and dogs. I like dogs but I don't like cats.
Interjection	short exclamation, sometimes inserted into a sentence	oh!, ouch!, hi!, well	Ouch! That hurts! Hi! How are you? Well, I don't know.

Words are assigned to parts of speech according to their grammatical behaviour. For example, words are classified according to the positions in which they can occur in a sentence and the way they change their forms for grammatical reasons.

Words placed together in a single part of speech have important grammatical properties in common, but that doesn't mean that all the words in a single part of speech have grammatical properties which are entirely identical.

In English, it is possible to assign a single word to two or more parts of speech. For example, book is a noun in the sentence 'Give me that book' but a verb in the sentence 'Book your tickets early'. Similarly fast is an adjective in the sequence 'a fast car' but an adverb in the sentence 'He drove fast'.

A few words exhibit behaviour that cannot be assigned to any part of speech at all. English examples include the negative 'not' and the polite 'please'.

■■■

CHAPTER 2

The Sentence

A sentence is the basic unit of written English language communication.

Simple Sentence

The basic English language sentence is called a simple sentence. It requires a subject and a verb. We ordinarily include some additional words that explain the subject. The sentence or a part of a sentence that contains a subject and a verb and constitutes a complete thought is called an independent clause.

For example, I like English.

The sentence above conveys a complete thought. The subject is I, and the verb is like. The word English conveys an understanding of what the subject likes. The sentence has one independent clause and is a simple sentence. Observe the arrangement or sequence of sentence components: subject, verb, other parts of the sentence. This arrangement is not mandatory, but sentences written in this format are usually easy to understand.

Complex Sentence

A complex sentence contains an independent clause and a

subordinate clause. The independent clause can function as a complete sentence. The subordinate clause also contains a subject and a verb but cannot function as an independent sentence.

For example: We surveyed the damage as the wind subsided.

We surveyed the damage. This is an independent clause and a complete sentence. The words convey a complete thought. The words as the wind subsided form a subordinate clause. The words do not convey an intelligent thought that can stand alone as a sentence. If we modify as the wind subsided so that it becomes The wind subsided, we realise that it contains both a subject and a verb. The words as the wind subsided constitute an adverbial expression that describes a condition that existed when we surveyed the damage.

Compound Sentence

A compound sentence contains two independent clauses. Two independent clauses may be joined by a comma and a conjunction, or by a semicolon, or by a colon.

The school year ends June 1st, but the sports programme will continue throughout the summer.

For example: We accept the design; it meets our standards.

The school board funded the computer laboratory; consequently, computer classes will be offered next year.

The judge has decided the case, and he ruled as follows, 'The court finds the defendant guilty and sentences him to time served.' You can write as many independent clauses and subordinate clauses into a single sentence as your imagination will support. However, reader comprehension declines as complexity increases.

Sentences may be classified according to the purpose of the sentence.

Sentence Classification by Purpose

Declarative Sentences

A declarative sentence is used to make a statement.

Examples: It's lunch time.

We are going to the game on Friday.

My car is out of gasoline.

My parents keep telling me that I should make good grades so I can get a job or go to college.

Interrogative Sentences

We frequently ask questions, perhaps not as frequently as we should. An interrogative sentence is used to pose a question.

Examples: What time does the movie start?

How many people from your graduating class went to college?

Is there a reason why these dirty clothes are in the middle of the floor?

What are they serving in the cafeteria today?

Imperative Sentences

People who have authority use imperative sentences. Sometimes, people who don't have authority use imperative sentences. The results may differ.

An imperative sentence is used to give a command or to implore or entreat.

Examples: Wash the car.

Clean up your room.

Mahesh, report to the counsellor.

Please donate to the community charity fund.

Exclamatory Sentences

An exclamatory sentence is used to express astonishment or extreme emotion. We say that sentences must have a subject and a verb. Note that some of the above sentences do not seem to have a subject. The subject is implied, and the implied subject is you. You wash the car. You clean up your room. You is a second person pronoun. It isn't possible to make a command statement in first person or third person.

Exclamatory sentences are rarely used in expository writing. Spoken exclamations are often a single word or an incomplete sentence. Grammarians indicate that formal exclamatory sentences begin with the word what or with the word how. Most of the exclamations we encounter are informal.

Examples: What a beautiful night!

How happy we were when the dawn came and our flag was still there!

What did you do to your hair! (exclamation formed as a question)

I just won 50,000 rupees! (exclamation formed as a declarative sentence)

More About Sentence Structure

The two fundamental parts of every English sentence are the subject and the predicate. A simple sentence can also be described as a group of words expressing a complete thought. Subjects can be described as the component that performs the action described by the Predicate.

SUBJECT + PREDICATE = SENTENCE

A simple sentence or independent clause must have a verb. A verb shows action or state of being. The subject tells who or what about the verb.

SUBJECT + VERB = SENTENCE

Sentence Structure Vocabulary

The sentence format consists of a subject and a predicate. The subject names the topic and the predicate tells about the subject.

A sentence with one subject and one predicate is called a simple sentence.

The receiver of actions is called the object.

A group of words used as a single value without subject or predicate is called a phrase.

A clause is a group of words with a subject and predicate.

Principal or independent clauses can form sentences.

A compound sentence contains two or more principal clauses.

A clause which cannot form a sentence is called a dependant clause.

A complex sentence contains a principal clause and one or more dependant or subordinate clauses.

A compound-complex sentence contains two principal clauses and one or more subordinate clauses.

The Six Basic Sentence Construction Patterns

1. *No Verb Complement:* The simplest structure is one without a verb complement. In traditional grammar, all verb complements are either nouns or adjectives.

   Examples 1. India wins.

2. *Direct Object Verb Complement:* The defining characteristic is the presence of a direct object.

   Example: Boys love cricket.

3. *Indirect and Direct Object Verb Complements:* Both indirect and direct objects are present. Indirect objects are placed

immediately after the verb. Direct objects that are noun phrases follow the indirect object.

Example: Dad gave [(me) (a bag)].

4. *Predicate Nominative Verb Complement:* The predicate nominative verb complement is a noun or a pronoun that redefines, renames, or classifies the subject of the sentence. The verb in a predicate nominative sentence pattern is always a linking verb, such as be, seem, or become.

   Example: He became a coach.

5. *Predicate Adjective Verb Complement:* The predicate adjective is an adjective that modifies the subject of the sentence. The verb is always a linking verb, such as be, seem, smell, look, taste, or become.

   Example: The game became difficult.

6. *Direct Object and Objective Complement:* The verb complements are a direct object and an objective complement. An objective complement is a noun or an adjective that occurs after the direct object and describes the direct object.

   Example: The class made [(me) (bilingual)].

Simple Sentences and Configurations

Simple Subject and Predicate

Example: Nita slept.

Understood subject (for commands, directives)

Example: Sit!

Questions

Example: What are you throwing?

Interjection

Example: Man, that hurt!

Compound predicate

Example: The bear howled and scratched ferociously.

Compound subject and predicate

Example: Meenu and Gaurav worked hard and then rested.

Three subjects

Example: Rahul, Himanshu, and Sheenu are working.

Direct object

Example: Piyush sent the letter.

Compound direct objects

Example: Tanu sent cards and letters.

Three direct objects

Example: Tanu sent posters, cards, and letters.

Compound predicate with direct objects

Example: Jessica cooked lunch and ate it.

Compound predicate with one direct object

Example: Sandhya proofreads and edits his essays.

Indirect object

Example: The teacher gave the children homework.

Compound indirect objects

Example: The teacher gave Sunny and Karan quizzes.

Predicate noun

Example: John is a coach.

Objective Complement

Example: Johnny painted his front porch white.

Direct address

Harish, tell the class now.

Adjective

Example: Athletic moves excite the crowd.

Compound adjectives

Example: The little old lady hit the tall and distinguished gentleman.

Predicate adjective

Example: The engine was powerful.

Compound predicate adjectives

Example: The engine was powerful but expensive.

Comparative Adjective

Example: Yash is considerably older than his brother.

Adverb

Example: Phagun works quickly.

Adverbs modifying other adverbs

Example: My dog wags its tail quite often.

Compound adverbs

Example: The cat waited patiently and quietly at the door.

Passive Verbs

Example: The ball was kicked.

■■■

CHAPTER 3

The Nouns

A noun is a word used to name a person, animal, place, thing, and abstract idea. Nouns are usually the first words which small children learn. Notice the nouns in the following sentences:

Late last year our neighbours bought a goat.

Gagan was a singer.

The bus inspector looked at all the passengers' passes.

According to Plutarch, the library at Alexandria was destroyed in 48 B.C.

Philosophy is of little comfort to the starving.

A noun can function in a sentence as a subject, a direct object, an indirect object, a subject complement, an object complement, an appositive, an adjective or an adverb.

Noun Gender

Many common nouns, like 'engineer' or 'teacher,' can refer to men or women. Once, many English nouns would change form depending on their gender — for example, a man was called an 'author' while a woman was called an 'authoress' — but this use of gender-specific nouns is very rare today. Those that are still used occasionally tend to refer to occupational categories, as in the following sentences.

Shahrukh Khan is a very prominent century actor.

The manager was trying to write a want ad, but he couldn't decide whether he was advertising for a 'waiter' or a 'waitress'

Noun Plurals

Most nouns change their form to indicate number by adding '-s' or '-es', as illustrated in the following pairs of sentences:

When Manu was small he rarely told the truth if he thought he was going to be punished.

Many people do not believe that truths are self-evident.

As they walked through the silent house, they were startled by an unexpected echo.

I like to shout into the quarry and listen to the echoes that return.

He tripped over a box left carelessly in the hallway.

Since we are moving, we will need many boxes.

There are other nouns which form the plural by changing the last letter before adding 's'. Some words ending in 'f' form the plural by deleting 'f' and adding 'ves,' and words ending in 'y' form the plural by deleting the 'y' and adding 'ies,' as in the following pairs of sentences:

The harbour at Marble Mountain has one wharf.

There are several wharves in Halifax Harbour.

Agra is their favourite city because it reminds them of their courtship.

The vacation my grandparents won includes trips to twelve European cities.

The children circled around the headmaster and shouted, 'Are you a mouse or a man?'

The audience was shocked when all five men admitted that they were afraid of mice.

Other nouns form the plural irregularly. If English is your first language, you probably know most of these already: when in doubt, consult a good dictionary.

Possessive Nouns

In the possessive case, a noun or pronoun changes its form to show that it owns or is closely related to something else. Usually, nouns become possessive by adding a combination of an apostrophe and the letter 's.'

You can form the possessive case of a singular noun that does not end in 's' by adding an apostrophe and 's,' as in the following sentences:

The red suitcase is Shruti's.

The only luggage that was lost was the sports minister's.

The exhausted recruits were woken before dawn by the drill sergeant's screams.

The miner's face was covered in coal dust.

You can form the possessive case of a singular noun that ends in 's' by adding an apostrophe alone or by adding an apostrophe and 's,' as in the following examples:

The bus's seats are very uncomfortable.

The bus' seats are very uncomfortable.

The film crew accidentally crushed the platypus's eggs.

The film crew accidentally crushed the platypus' eggs.

You can form the possessive case of a plural noun that does not end in 's' by adding an apostrophe and a 's,' as in the following examples:

The children's mittens were scattered on the floor of the porch.

The sheep's pen was mucked out every day.

Since we have a complex appeal process, a jury's verdict is not always final.

The men's hockey team will be playing as soon as the women's team is finished.

The hunter followed the moose's trail all morning but lost it in the afternoon.

You can form the possessive case of a plural noun that does end in 's' by adding an apostrophe:

The concert was interrupted by the dogs' barking, the ducks' quacking, and the babies' squalling.

The janitors' room is downstairs and to the left.

My uncle spent many hours trying to locate the squirrels' nest.

The archivist quickly finished repairing the diaries' bindings.

Religion is usually the subject of the roommates' many late night debates.

Using Possessive Nouns

When you read the following sentences, you will notice that a noun in the possessive case frequently functions as an adjective modifying another noun:

The miner's face was covered in coal dust.

Here the possessive noun 'miner's' is used to modify the noun 'face' and together with the article 'the,' they make up the noun phrase that is the sentence's subject.

The concert was interrupted by the dogs' barking, the ducks' quacking, and the babies' squalling.

In this sentence, each possessive noun modifies a gerund. The possessive noun 'dogs'' modifies 'barking,' 'ducks'' modifies 'quacking,' and 'babies'' modifies 'squalling.'

The film crew accidentally crushed the platypus's eggs.

In this example the possessive noun 'platypus's' modifies

the noun 'eggs' and the noun phrase 'the platypus's eggs' is the direct object of the verb 'crushed.'

Types of Nouns

There are many different types of nouns. As you know, you capitalise some nouns, such as 'Canada' or 'Kerala,' and do not capitalise others, such as 'badger' or 'tree' (unless they appear at the beginning of a sentence). In fact, grammarians have developed a whole series of noun types, including the proper noun, the common noun, the concrete noun, the abstract noun, the countable noun (also called the count noun), the non-countable noun (also called the mass noun), and the collective noun. You should note that a noun will belong to more than one type: it will be proper or common, abstract or concrete, and countable or non-countable or collective.

If you are interested in the details of these different types, you can read about them in the following sections.

Proper Nouns

You always write a proper noun with a capital letter, since the noun represents the name of a specific person, place, or thing. The names of days of the week, months, historical documents, institutions, organisations, religions, their holy texts and their adherents are proper nouns. A proper noun is the opposite of a common noun

Notice the proper nouns here:

Many people dread Monday mornings.

Abraham appears in the Talmud and in the Koran.

Last year, I had a Baptist, a Buddhist, and a Gardnerian Witch as roommates.

Common Nouns

A common noun is a noun referring to a person, place, or thing in a general sense — usually, you should write it with a capital letter only when it begins a sentence. A common noun is the opposite of a proper noun.

In each of the following sentences, notice the common nouns:

According to the sign, the nearest town is 60 miles away.

All the gardens in the neighbourhood were invaded by beetles this summer.

I don't understand why some people insist on having six different kinds of mustard in their cupboards.

The road crew was startled by the sight of three large moose crossing the road.

Many child-care workers are underpaid.

Sometimes you will make proper nouns out of common nouns, as in the following examples:

Many witches refer to the Renaissance as the Burning Times.

The Diary of Anne Frank is often a child's first introduction to the history of the Holocaust.

Concrete Nouns

A concrete noun is a noun which names anything (or anyone) that you can perceive through your physical senses: touch, sight, taste, hearing, or smell. A concrete noun is the opposite of an abstract noun.

Notice theconcrete nouns in the following sentences here:

The judge handed the files to the clerk.

Whenever they take the dog to the beach, it spends hours chasing waves.

The real estate agent urged the couple to buy the second house because it had new shingles.

As the car drove past the park, the thump of a disco tune overwhelmed the string quartets rendition of a minuet.

The book binder replaced the flimsy paper cover with a sturdy, cloth-covered board.

Abstract Nouns

An abstract noun is a noun which names anything which you can not perceive through your five physical senses, and is the opposite of a concrete noun. Notice the abstract nouns in the following sentences:

Buying the fire extinguisher was an afterthought.

Honey is amused by people who are nostalgic about childhood.

Justice often seems to slip out of our grasp.

Some scientists believe that schizophrenia is transmitted genetically.

Countable Nouns

A countable noun (or count noun) is a noun with both a singular and a plural form, and it names anything (or anyone) that you can count. You can make a countable noun plural and attach it to a plural verb in a sentence. Countable nouns are the opposite of non-countable nouns and collective nouns.

Notice the use of countable nouns here:

We painted the table red and the chairs blue.

Since he inherited his aunt's library, Gautam spends every weekend indexing his books.

Megha found six silver coins in the toe of a sock.

The oak tree lost three branches in the hurricane.

Over the course of twenty-seven years, Dr. Sarita delivered just over eight hundred babies.

Non-Countable Nouns

A non-countable noun (or mass noun) is a noun which does not have a plural form, and which refers to something that you could (or would) not usually count. A non-countable noun always takes a singular verb in a sentence. Non-countable nouns are similar to collective nouns, and are the opposite of countable nouns.

Notice the non-countable nouns in these sentences:

Joseph Priestly discovered oxygen.

The word 'oxygen' cannot normally be made plural.

Oxygen is essential to human life.

Since 'oxygen' is a non-countable noun, it takes the singular verb 'is' rather than the plural verb 'are.'

We decided to sell the furniture rather than take it with us when we moved.

You cannot make the noun 'furniture' plural.

The furniture is heaped in the middle of the room.

Since 'furniture' is a non-countable noun, it takes a singular verb, 'is heaped.'

The crew spread the gravel over the roadbed.

You cannot make the non-countable noun 'gravel' plural.

Gravel is more expensive than I thought.

Since 'gravel' is a non-countable noun, it takes the singular verb form 'is.'

Collective Nouns

A collective noun is a noun naming a group of things, animals, or persons. You could count the individual members of the group, but you usually think of the group as a whole is generally as one unit. You need to be able to recognise collective nouns in order to maintain subject-verb agreement. A collective noun is similar to a non-countable noun, and is roughly the opposite of a countable noun.

Notice collective nouns in these sentences:

The flock of geese spends most of its time in the pasture.

The collective noun 'flock' takes the singular verb 'spends.'

The jury is dining on take-out chicken tonight.

In this example the collective noun 'jury' is the subject of the singular compound verb 'is dining.'

The steering committee meets every Wednesday afternoon.

Here the collective noun 'committee' takes a singular verb, 'meets.'

The class was startled by the bursting light bulb.

In this sentence the word 'class' is a collective noun and takes the singular compound verb 'was startled.'

CHAPTER 4

Pronoun

A pronoun can replace a noun or another pronoun. You use pronouns like 'he,' 'which,' 'none,' and 'you' to make your sentences less cumbersome and less repetitive.

Grammarians classify pronouns into several types, including the personal pronoun, the demonstrative pronoun, the interrogative pronoun, the indefinite pronoun, the relative pronoun, the reflexive pronoun, and the intensive pronoun.

Personal Pronouns

A personal pronoun refers to a specific person or thing and changes its form to indicate person, number, gender, and case.

Subjective Personal Pronouns

A subjective personal pronoun indicates that the pronoun is acting as the subject of the sentence. The subjective personal pronouns are 'I,' 'you,' 'she,' 'he,' 'it,' 'we,' 'you,' 'they.'

In the following sentences, notice the subjective personal pronouns and see how they act as the subject of the sentence:

I was glad to find the bus pass in the bottom of the green knapsack.

You are surely the strangest child I have ever met.

He stole the Manisha's skin and forced her to live with him.

When she was a young woman, she earned her living as a coal miner.

After many years, they returned to their homeland.

We will meet at the library at 3:30 p.m.

It is on the counter.

Are you the delegates from Malagawatch?

Objective Personal Pronouns

An objective personal pronoun indicates that the pronoun is acting as an object of a verb, compound verb, preposition, or infinitive phrase. The objective personal pronouns are: 'me,' 'you,' 'her,' 'him,' 'it,' 'us,' 'you,' and 'them.'

In the following sentences, notice the use of objective personal pronoun:

Harish stole the Manisha's skin and forced her to live with him.

The objective personal pronoun 'her' is the direct object of the verb 'forced' and the objective personal pronoun 'him' is the object of the preposition 'with.'

After reading the pamphlet, Judy threw it into the garbage can.

The pronoun 'it' is the direct object of the verb 'threw.'

The agitated assistant stood up and faced the angry delegates and said, 'Our leader will address you in five minutes.'

In this sentence, the pronoun 'you' is the direct object of the verb 'address.'

Parul and Ravina will meet us at the newest café in the market.

Here the objective personal pronoun 'us' is the direct object of the compound verb 'will meet.'

Give the list to me.

Here the objective personal pronoun 'me' is the object of the preposition 'to.'

I'm not sure that my contact will talk to you.

Similarly in this example, the objective personal pronoun 'you' is the object of the preposition 'to.'

Karan was surprised to see her at the drag races.

Here the objective personal pronoun 'her' is the object of the infinitive phrase 'to see.'

Possessive Personal Pronouns

A possessive pronoun indicates that the pronoun is acting as a marker of possession and defines who owns a particular object or person. The possessive personal pronouns are 'mine,' 'yours,' 'hers,' 'his,' 'its,' 'ours,' and 'theirs.' Note that possessive personal pronouns are very similar to possessive adjectives like 'my,' 'her,' and 'their.'

In each of the following sentences, notice the possessive personal pronouns:

The smallest gift is mine.

Here the possessive pronoun 'mine' functions as a subject complement.

This is yours.

Here too the possessive pronoun 'yours' functions as a subject complement.

His is on the kitchen counter.

In this example, the possessive pronoun 'his' acts as the subject of the sentence.

Theirs will be delivered tomorrow.

In this sentence, the possessive pronoun 'theirs' is the subject of the sentence.

Ours is the green one on the corner.

Here too the possessive pronoun 'ours' function as the subject of the sentence.

Demonstrative Pronouns

A demonstrative pronoun points to and identifies a noun or a pronoun. 'This' and 'these' refer to things that are nearby either in space or in time, while 'that' and 'those' refer to things that are farther away in space or time.

The demonstrative pronouns are 'this,' 'that,' 'these,' and 'those.' 'This' and 'that' are used to refer to singular nouns or noun phrases and 'these' and 'those' are used to refer to plural nouns and noun phrases.

Note that the demonstrative pronouns are identical to demonstrative adjectives, though, obviously, you use them differently. It is also important to note that 'that' can also be used as a relative pronoun.

In the following sentences, notice the use of demonstrative pronouns:

This must not continue.

Here 'this' is used as the subject of the compound verb 'must not continue.'

This is puny; that is the tree I want.

In this example 'this' is used as subject and refers to something close to the speaker. The demonstrative pronoun 'that' is also a subject but refers to something farther away from the speaker.

Three customers wanted these.

Here 'these' is the direct object of the verb 'wanted.'

Interrogative Pronouns

An interrogative pronoun is used to ask questions. The interrogative pronouns are 'who,' 'whom,' 'which,' 'what' and the compounds formed with the suffix 'ever' ('whoever,' 'whomever,' 'whichever,' and 'whatever'). Note that either 'which' or 'what' can also be used as an interrogative adjective, and that 'who,' 'whom,' or 'which' can also be used as a relative pronoun.

You will find 'who,' 'whom,' and occasionally 'which' used to refer to people, and 'which' and 'what' used to refer to things and to animals.

'Who' acts as the subject of a verb, while 'whom' acts as the object of a verb, preposition, or a verbal.

Notice th euse of interrogative pronouns in these sentences:

Which wants to see the dentist first?

'Which' is the subject of the sentence.

Who wrote the novel Rockbound?

Similarly 'who' is the subject of the sentence.

Whom do you think we should invite?

In this sentence, 'whom' is the object of the verb 'invite.'

To whom do you wish to speak?

Here the interrogative pronoun 'whom ' is the object of the preposition 'to.'

Who will meet the delegates at the train station?

In this sentence, the interrogative pronoun 'who' is the subject of the compound verb 'will meet.'

To whom did you give the paper?

In this example the interrogative pronoun 'whom' is the object of the preposition 'to.'

What did she say?

Here the interrogative pronoun 'what' is the direct object of the verb 'say.'

Relative Pronouns

You can use a relative pronoun is used to link one phrase or clause to another phrase or clause. The relative pronouns are 'who,' 'whom,' 'that,' and 'which.' The compounds 'whoever,' 'whomever,' and 'whichever' are also relative pronouns.

You can use the relative pronouns 'who' and 'whoever' to refer to the subject of a clause or sentence, and 'whom' and 'whomever' to refer to the objects of a verb, a verbal or a preposition.

Notice the use of relative pronouns in these sentences:

You may invite whomever you like to the party.

The relative pronoun 'whomever' is the direct object of the compound verb 'may invite.'

The candidate who wins the greatest popular vote is not always elected.

In this sentence, the relative pronoun is the subject of the verb 'wins' and introduces the subordinate clause 'who wins the greatest popular vote.' This subordinate clause acts as an adjective modifying 'candidate.'

In a time of crisis, the manager asks the workers whom she believes to be the most efficient to arrive an hour earlier than usual.

In this sentence 'whom' is the direct object of the verb 'believes' and introduces the subordinate clause 'whom she believes to be the most efficient'. This subordinate clause modifies the noun 'workers.'

Whoever broke the window will have to replace it.

Here 'whoever' functions as the subject of the verb 'broke.'

The crate which was left in the corridor has now been moved into the storage closet.

In this example 'which' acts as the subject of the compound verb 'was left' and introduces the subordinate clause 'which was left in the corridor.' The subordinate clause acts as an adjective modifying the noun 'crate.'

I will read whichever manuscript arrives first.

Here 'whichever' modifies the noun 'manuscript' and introduces the subordinate clause 'whichever manuscript arrives first.' The subordinate clause functions as the direct object of the compound verb 'will read.'

Indefinite Pronouns

An indefinite pronoun is a pronoun referring to an identifiable but not specified person or thing. An indefinite pronoun conveys the idea of all, any, none, or some.

The most common indefinite pronouns are 'all,' 'another,' 'any,' 'anybody,' 'anyone,' 'anything,' 'each,' 'everybody,' 'everyone,' 'everything,' 'few,' 'many,' 'nobody,' 'none,' 'one,' 'several,' 'some,' 'somebody,' and 'someone.' Note that some indefinite pronouns can also be used as indefinite adjectives.

In the the following sentences, see the use of indefinite pronouns:

Many were invited to the lunch but only twelve showed up.

Here 'many' acts as the subject of the compound verb 'were invited.'

The office had been searched and everything was thrown onto the floor.

In this example, 'everything' acts as a subject of the compound verb 'was thrown.'

We donated everything we found in the attic to the woman's shelter garage sale.

In this sentence, 'everything' is the direct object of the verb 'donated.'

Give a registration package to each.

Here 'each' is the object of the preposition 'to.'

Reflexive Pronouns

You can use a reflexive pronoun to refer back to the subject of the clause or sentence.

The reflexive pronouns are 'myself,' 'yourself,' 'herself,' 'himself,' 'itself,' 'ourselves,' 'yourselves,' and 'themselves.' Note each of these can also act as an intensive pronoun.

Notice the use of reflexive pronouns here:

Diabetics give themselves insulin shots several times a day.

The Dean often does the photocopying herself so that the secretaries can do more important work.

After the party, I asked myself why I had faxed invitations to everyone in my office building.

Raghu usually remembered to send a copy of his e-mail to himself.

Although the landlord promised to paint the apartment, we ended up doing it ourselves.

Intensive Pronouns

An intensive pronoun is a pronoun used to emphasise its antecedent. Intensive pronouns are identical in form to reflexive pronouns.

Notice the use of intensive pronouns in these sentences:

I myself believe that aliens should abduct my sister.

The Prime Minister himself said that he would lower taxes.

They themselves promised to come to the party even though they had a final exam at the same time.

There are several categories of pronouns, but they all replace nouns in a sentence. The following lists include the most commonly used pronouns.

Personal	Possessive	Relative	Reflexive
I	His	Who	Myself
Me	Hers	Whose	Yourself
He	Its	That	Himself
She	Yours	Which	Herself
It	Ours	Whoever	Ourselves
Him	Theirs	Whichever	Themselves
Her	Whatever		
You			
We			
They			
Them			

CHAPTER 5

The Adjective

An adjective modifies a noun or a pronoun by describing, identifying, or quantifying words. An adjective usually precedes the noun or the pronoun which it modifies.

In the following examples, notice the adjectives used:

The truck-shaped balloon floated over the treetops.

Mrs. Sharma papered her kitchen walls with hideous wall paper.

The small boat foundered on the wine dark sea.

The coal mines are dark and dank.

Many stores have already begun to play irritating Christmas music.

A battered music box sat on the mahogany sideboard.

The back room was filled with large, yellow rain boots.

An adjective can be modified by an adverb, or by a phrase or clause functioning as an adverb. In the sentence

My husband knits intricately patterned mittens.

For example, the adverb 'intricately' modifies the adjective 'patterned.'

Some nouns, many pronouns, and many participle phrases can also act as adjectives. In the sentence

Eleanor listened to the muffled sounds of the radio hidden under her pillow.

For example, 'muffled' and 'radio hidden' are past participles.

Grammarians also consider articles ('the,' 'a,' 'an') to be adjectives.

Possessive Adjectives

A possessive adjective ('my,' 'your,' 'his,' 'her,' 'its,' 'our,' 'their') is similar or identical to a possessive pronoun; however, it is used as an adjective and modifies a noun or a noun phrase, as in the following sentences:

I can't complete my assignment because I don't have the textbook.

In this sentence, the possessive adjective 'my' modifies 'assignment' and the noun phrase 'my assignment' functions as an object. Note that the possessive pronoun form 'mine' is not used to modify a noun or noun phrase.

What is your phone number?

Here the possessive adjective 'your' is used to modify the noun phrase 'phone number'; the entire noun phrase 'your phone number' is a subject complement. Note that the possessive pronoun form 'yours' is not used to modify a noun or a noun phrase.

The bakery sold his favourite type of bread.

In this example, the possessive adjective 'his' modifies the noun phrase 'favourite type of bread' and the entire noun phrase 'his favourite type of bread' is the direct object of the verb 'sold.'

After many years, she returned to her homeland.

Here the possessive adjective 'her' modifies the noun 'homeland' and the noun phrase 'her homeland' is the object of the preposition 'to.' Note also that the form 'hers' is not used to modify nouns or noun phrases.

We have lost our way in this wood.

In this sentence, the possessive adjective 'our' modifies 'way' and the noun phrase 'our way' is the direct object of the compound verb 'have lost'. Note that the possessive pronoun form 'ours' is not used to modify nouns or noun phrases.

In many fairy tales, children are neglected by their parents.

Here the possessive adjective 'their' modifies 'parents' and the noun phrase 'their parents' is the object of the preposition 'by.' Note that the possessive pronoun form 'theirs' is not used to modify nouns or noun phrases.

The cat chased its ball down the stairs and into the backyard.

In this sentence, the possessive adjective 'its' modifies 'ball' and the noun phrase 'its ball' is the object of the verb 'chased.' Note that 'its' is the possessive adjective and 'it's' is a contraction for 'it is.'

Demonstrative Adjectives

The demonstrative adjectives 'this,' 'these,' 'that,' 'those,' and 'what' are identical to the demonstrative pronouns, but are used as adjectives to modify nouns or noun phrases, as in the following sentences:

When the librarian tripped over that cord, she dropped a pile of books.

In this sentence, the demonstrative adjective 'that' modifies the noun 'cord' and the noun phrase 'that cord' is the object of the preposition 'over.'

This apartment needs to be fumigated.

Here 'this' modifies 'apartment' and the noun phrase 'this apartment' is the subject of the sentence.

Even though my friend preferred those plates, I bought these.

In the subordinate clause, 'those' modifies 'plates' and the noun phrase 'those plates' is the object of the verb 'preferred.' In the independent clause, 'these' is the direct object of the verb 'bought.'

Interrogative Adjectives

An interrogative adjective ('which' or 'what') is like an interrogative pronoun, except that it modifies a noun or noun phrase rather than standing on its own (see also demonstrative adjectives and possessive adjectives):

Which plants should be watered twice a week?

Like other adjectives, 'which' can be used to modify a noun or a noun phrase. In this example, 'which' modifies 'plants' and the noun phrase 'which plants' is the subject of the compound verb 'should be watered':

What book are you reading?

In this sentence, 'what' modifies 'book' and the noun phrase 'what book' is the direct object of the compound verb 'are reading.'

Indefinite Adjectives

An indefinite adjective is similar to an indefinite pronoun, except that it modifies a noun, pronoun, or noun phrase, as in the following sentences:

Many people believe that corporations are under-taxed.

The indefinite adjective 'many' modifies the noun 'people' and the noun phrase 'many people' is the subject of the sentence.

I will send you any mail that arrives after you have moved to Sudbury.

The indefinite adjective 'any' modifies the noun 'mail' and the noun phrase 'any mail' is the direct object of the compound verb 'will send.'

They found a few goldfish floating belly up in the swan pound.

In this example the indefinite adjective modifies the noun 'goldfish' and the noun phrase is the direct object of the verb 'found':

The title of Kelly's favourite game is 'All dogs go to heaven.'

Here the indefinite pronoun 'all' modifies 'dogs' and the full title is a subject complement.

CHAPTER 6

Verb

A verb is a word used to tell or assert something about some person or thing.

The verb is perhaps the most important part of the sentence. A verb or compound verb asserts something about the subject of the sentence and express actions, events, or states of being. The verb or compound verb is the critical element of the predicate of a sentence.

In each of the following sentences notice the use of verbs:

Dracula bites his victims on the neck.

The verb 'bites' describes the action Dracula takes.

In early October, Garima will plant twenty tulip bulbs.

Here the compound verb 'will plant' describes an action that will take place in the future.

My first teacher was Miss Tina, but I remember the janitor Mr. Verma more vividly.

In this sentence, the verb 'was' (the simple past tense of 'is') identifies a particular person and the verb 'remembered' describes a mental action.

Karl Creelman bicycled around the world in 1899, but his diaries and his bicycle were destroyed.

In this sentence, the compound verb 'were destroyed' describes an action which took place in the past.

The Verb is a word or phrase that indicates what somebody or something does, what state somebody or something is in, what is becoming of something or somebody. Check these sentences:

1. A fly caves cholera.
2. Flies fly over dirty things.

   In the first sentence, 'fly' is a noun, in the second sentence, 'fly' is a verb.

   A verb always agrees with its subjects.

   Before you know the details about verbs, please pay attention to the singular and plural forms of verb and their agreement with their subjects.

1. Singular Number: The base form of all the verbs with the suffix 's, es' – Worships, helps, goes, runs, walks, plays, studies, files, educates, vanishes, cleans, walks, talks, whitewashes, digs, chooses, elects, selects, etc.
2. Plural Number: The base form of all the verbs without any suffix - help, walk, talk, worship, study, read, wife, wash, computerize, relative, select, elect, etc.
3. I & You always take the plural form of verbs – help, walk, talk, teach, private, arrange, gather, hold, admire, praise, appreciate, etc.
4. Singular – is, was, has, appreciates, does.
5. Plural – are, were, have, do, appreciate.
6. I – am, was, have, do, appreciate.
7. You – are, were, have, do, appreciate.

The other terms of verb are used in the singular, in the plural as well.

Transitive Verbs

A transitive verb is a verb that denotes an action which passes over from the subject to an object.

1. The boy bought a book.
2. She sang a melodious song.

 Some transitive verbs take two objects after them. They are:

(i) an indirect object, it demotes the person to whom something is given or for whom something is done.

(ii)direct object it is usually the name of something.

 Study these sentences:

1. The teacher gave me a book.
2. The teacher gave a book to me.

 In both the sentences, 'me' is an indirect and 'book' is a direct object. Prepositions (to, for) must be placed if the indirect object comes after the direct object.

Study more examples:

1. I sent my friend a letter.
2. He owed me one hundred rupee.
3. My friend did me a great kindness.
4. The principal gave the bright boy a prize.
5. I bought my son a car.

Check these again:

1. I sent a letter to my son.
2. He owed one hundred rupees to me.

3. My friend did a great kindness to me.
4. The principal gave a prize to the bright boy.
5. I brought a car for my son.

Intransitive Verbs

An intransitive verb is a verb that denotes an action which does not pass over to an object or which expresses a state of being. For example:

1. I go for a walk.
2. My grandchild hardly sleeps in the day.
3. The train was running at very high speed.
4. The child was weeping.
5. We live happily.

Linking Verbs

A few verbs express a static condition or state of being (no action). Most of these inactive verbs are called linking verbs; such verbs are called verbs of incomplete predication. They require some complements to make such sentences complete.

Such verbs are – to be, is , am, are, was, were, become, grow, go, come, run, small, taste, appears, seen, took, make, get, etc.

Note: Some of these linking verbs do not require any complement to make the sense complete, hence, they are not linking verbs.

1. The boys looked by happy.
2. The boys looked at monkeys.

In the first sentence, 'looked' is the verb of incomplete predicate and takes 'happy' for the complete sense. In the second sentence, 'looked' does not require any complement for the complete sentence and is 'an action verb'.

Complements: The words that complete the sense of the verbs of incomplete predicative are called complements. They are – noun complements, adjectival complements, adverbial complements, participle complements, geined complement, phrasal complete.

Study the following sentence – with subjective complement –

1. He was great. (adjectival complement)
2. The dog went mad. (adjectival complement)
3. She remained rich all her life. (adjectival complement)
4. Your guess went wrong. (adjectival complement)

Objective Complements:

1. We made him president.
2. I found the child asleep.
3. The judge sentenced the prisoner to be hanger.
4. I found my friend worried.
5. We judge him great.

Note: Some transitive verbs require, besides an object, a complement. Study the following sentences:

1. The boys run fast.
2. Some rivers run dry in summer.
3. She went to school.
4. He made a chair.
5. He made his mother happy.
6. Her guess went wrong.

Transitive Verbs:

1. The children are flying kites in the sky.
2. Farmers grow rice and wheat in the fields.

3. That businessman runs many factories.
4. The sailors flouted their boats.
5. The driver stopped the bus and we all alighted.

Types of Verbs

Before you begin the verb tense lessons, it is extremely important to understand that NOT all English verbs are the same. English verbs are divided into three groups: Normal Verbs, Non-Continuous Verbs, and Mixed Verbs.

Group I Normal Verbs

Most verbs are 'Normal Verbs.' These verbs are usually physical actions which you can see somebody doing. These verbs can be used in all tenses.

Normal Verbs

to run, to walk, to eat, to fly, to go, to say, to touch, etc.

Examples:

I eat dinner every day.

I am eating dinner now.

Group II Non-Continuous Verbs

The second group, called 'Non-Continuous Verbs,' is smaller. These verbs are usually things you cannot see somebody doing. These verbs are rarely used in continuous tenses. They include:

Abstract Verbs

to be, to want, to cost, to seem, to need, to care, to contain, to owe, to exist...

Possession Verbs

to possess, to own, to belong...

Emotion Verbs

to like, to love, to hate, to dislike, to fear, to envy, to mind...

Examples:

He is needing help now. Not Correct

He needs help now. Correct

He is wanting a drink now. Not Correct

He wants a drink now. Correct

Mixed Verbs

The third group, called 'Mixed Verbs,' is the smallest group. These verbs have more than one meaning. In a way, each meaning is a unique verb. Some meanings behave like 'Non-Continuous Verbs,' while other meanings behave like 'Normal Verbs.'

Mixed Verbs

to appear, to feel, to have, to hear, to look, to see, to weigh...

List of Mixed Verbs with Examples and Definitions:

to appear:

Donna appears confused. Non-Continuous Verb

Donna seems confused.

My favourite singer is appearing at the jazz club tonight. Normal Verb

My favourite singer is giving a performance at the jazz club tonight.

to have:

I have a dollar now. Non-Continuous Verb

I possess a dollar.

Chapter 7

Adverb

An adverb is a word that tells us more about a verb. It 'qualifies' or 'modifies' a verb (The man ran quickly). Notice the adverbs in the following examples:

Jimmy speaks loudly. (How does Jimmy speak?)

Afterwards he smoked a cigarette. (When did he smoke?)

Manisha lives locally. (Where does Manisha live?)

But adverbs can also modify adjectives (Tara is really beautiful), or even other adverbs (It works very well). Look at these examples:

Modify an adjective:

- He is really handsome. (How handsome is he?)
- That was extremely kind of you.

Modify another adverb:

- She drives incredibly slowly. (How slowly does she drive?)
- He drives extremely fast.

We make many adverbs by adding -ly to an adjective, for example:

quick (adjective) > quickly (adverb)
careful (adjective) > carefully (adverb)
beautiful (adjective) > beautifully (adverb)

Kinds of Adverbs

Adverbs of Manner

Adverbs of Manner tell us the manner or way in which something happens. They answer the question 'how?'. Adverbs of Manner mainly modify verbs.

He speaks slowly. (How does he speak?)

They helped us cheerfully. (How did they help us?)

James Bond drives his cars fast. (How does James Bond drive his cars?)

We normally use Adverbs of Manner with dynamic (action) verbs, not with stative or state verbs.

He ran fast. She came quickly. They worked happily.

She looked beautifully. It seems strangely. They are happily.

Adverbs of Manner List

Adverbs of manner form the largest group of adverbs. We make most of them simply by adding -ly to their corresponding adjective. This is an alphabetical list of 130 common single-word adverbs of manner. Adverbs of manner that do not end in -ly are shown in bold.

accidentally angrily anxiously
awkwardly badly beautifully
blindly boldly bravely
brightly busily calmly
carefully carelessly cautiously
cheerfully clearly closely
correctly courageously cruelly

daringly	deliberately	doubtfully
eagerly	easily	elegantly
enormously	enthusiastically	equally
eventually	exactly	faithfully
fast	fatally	fiercely
fondly	foolishly	fortunately
frankly	frantically	generously
gently	gladly	gracefully
greedily	happily	hard
hastily	healthily	honestly
hungrily	hurriedly	inadequately
ingeniously	innocently	inquisitively
irritably	joyously	justly
kindly	lazily	loosely
loudly	madly	mortally
mysteriously	neatly	nervously
noisily	obediently	openly
painfully	patiently	perfectly
politely	poorly	powerfully
promptly	punctually	quickly
quietly	rapidly	rarely
really	recklessly	regularly
reluctantly	repeatedly	rightfully
roughly	rudely	sadly
safely	selfishly	sensibly
seriously	sharply	shyly
silently	sleepily	slowly
smoothly	so	softly

solemnly	speedily	stealthily
sternly	straight	stupidly
successfully	suddenly	suspiciously
swiftly	tenderly	tensely
thoughtfully	tightly	truthfully
unexpectedly	victoriously	violently
vivaciously	warmly	weakly
wearily	well	wildly

Adverbs of Place

Adverbs of Place tell us the place where something happens. They answer the question 'where?'. Adverbs of Place mainly modify verbs.

Please sit here. (Where should I sit?)

They looked everywhere. (Where did they look?)

Two cars were parked outside. (Where were two cars parked?)

Adverbs of Place List

Alphabetical list of common single-word place adverbs

about	above
abroad	anywhere
away	back
backwards (also backward)	behind
below	down
downstairs	east (etc)
elsewhere	far
here	in
indoors	inside
near	nearby

off	on
out	outside
over	there
towards	under
up	upstairs

Common Suffixes

- wards or -ward (backwards, downwards, eastward, forwards, homewards, upwards)
- where (anywhere

Adverbs of Time

Adverbs of Time tell us something about the time that something happens. Adverbs of Time mainly modify verbs.

- They can answer the question 'when?':
- He came yesterday. (When did he come?)
- I want it now. (When do I want it?)

Adverbs of time list

points of time (definite):

now	then
today	tomorrow
tonight	yesterday

frequency (definite):

annually	daily
fortnightly	hourly
monthly	nightly
quarterly	weekly

The word 'bio-monthly' is ambiguous and best avoided.

Bio-monthly can mean 'twice a month' or 'every two months'. The same is true of 'biyearly'/'biannually'.

frequency (indefinite):

always	constantly
ever	frequently
generally	infrequently
never	normally
occasionally	often
rarely	regularly
seldom	sometimes
regularly	usually

relationships in time (indefinite):

already	before
early	earlier
eventually	finally
first	formerly
just	last
late	later
lately	next
previously	recently
since	soon

Adverbs of Degree

Adverbs of Degree tell us the degree or extent to which something happens. They answer the question 'how much?' or 'to what degree?'. Adverbs of Degree can modify verbs, adjectives and other adverbs.

She entirely agrees with him. (How much does she agree with him?)

Manisha is very beautiful. (To what degree is Manisha beautiful? How beautiful is Manisha?)

He drove quite dangerously. (To what degree did he drive dangerously? How dangerously did he drive?)

Adverbs of Degree List

almost	absolutely	awfully
badly	barely	completely
decidedly	deeply	enough
enormously	entirely	extremely
fairly	far	fully
greatly	hardly	highly
how	incredibly	indeed
intensely	just	least
less	little	lots
most	much	nearly
perfectly	positively	practically
pretty*	purely	quite
rather	really	scarcely
simply	so	somewhat
strongly	terribly	thoroughly
too	totally	utterly
very	virtually	well

Adverb Position

When an adverb modifies a verb, there are usually 3 possible positions within the sentence or clause:

1. FRONT - before subject		Now	I will read a book.
2. MID - between subject + verb	I	often	read books.
3. END - after verb/object	I read books	carefully.	

When an adverb modifies an adjective or another adverb, it usually goes in front of the word that it modifies, for example:

	adverb	**adjective**	
She gave him a	really	dirty	look.
	adverb	adverb	
We	quite	often	study English.

The position of an adverb often depends on the kind of adverb (manner, place, time, degree). The following table gives you some guidelines for placement based on the kind of adverb.

Note: These are guidelines only. There are many exceptions.

<table>
<tr><th colspan="2" rowspan="2">kind of adverb</th><th rowspan="2">mainly modifies</th><th colspan="3">Sentence</th><th rowspan="2">usual position</th></tr>
<tr><th></th><th>adverb</th><th></th></tr>
<tr><td colspan="2">manner</td><td>verbs</td><td>She stroked his hair</td><td>gently.</td><td></td><td>END</td></tr>
<tr><td colspan="2">place</td><td>verbs</td><td>He was working</td><td>here.</td><td></td><td>END</td></tr>
<tr><td rowspan="2">time</td><td>definite</td><td rowspan="2">verbs</td><td>He finished the job</td><td>yester-day.</td><td></td><td>END</td></tr>
<tr><td>freque-ncy</td><td>We</td><td>often</td><td>go to Paris.</td><td>MID</td></tr>
<tr><td colspan="2" rowspan="3">degree</td><td rowspan="3">verbs, adjectiv-es and adverbs</td><td>I</td><td>nearly</td><td>died.</td><td>MID</td></tr>
<tr><td>It was</td><td>terribly</td><td>funny.</td><td>before adjective</td></tr>
<tr><td>He works</td><td>really</td><td>fast.</td><td>before adverb</td></tr>
</table>

Chapter 8

Preposition

Prepositions are relationship or directional words. They link the nouns, pronouns, verbs and phrases together in a sentence. Without prepositions, it would be impossible to understand communication. For example, would you understand a sentence that read: 'I want go the mall get a dress prom.' Perhaps you might be able to decipher it, but it certainly wouldn't be too fun. The missing words in that example are prepositions (to and for to be exact) and there are plenty more prepositions where that came.

The words at, in, of, on and to are examples of prepositions. A word such as a noun, pronoun or gerund following a preposition is said to be the object of the preposition. As pointed out previously, a personal pronoun following a preposition must be in the objective case.

A phrase beginning with a preposition can be referred to as a prepositional phrase. The prepositional phrases in the following examples are underlined.

E.g. He owns the house on the corner.

We are waiting for her.

She has read many books about flying.

In the first example, the noun corner is the object of the preposition on. In the second example, the personal pronoun her is the object of the preposition for. It can be seen that the personal pronoun her is in the objective case. In the third example, the gerund flying is the object of the preposition about.

A preposition serves to connect its object with the rest of a sentence. In doing so, a preposition indicates the relationship of the idea expressed in the prepositional phrase to the ideas expressed In the rest of the sentence.

For instance in the sentence He owns the house on the corner, the preposition on indicates that the words the corner express the location of the house referred to in the rest of the sentence. Similarly, in the sentence We are waiting for her, the preposition for indicates that the word her expresses the reason for the action of waiting referred to in the rest of the sentence.

The table below gives the most usual meanings of English prepositions. Each meaning is illustrated by an example.

About

1. On the subject of: This is a story about elephants.
2. Approximately: He is about ten years old.

Above

1. Higher than; over: The plane flew above the clouds.
2. Earlier on a page: There is a heading above each diagram.

Across

1. From one side to the other: We walked across the field.
2. On the other side of: There is a store across the street.

After

1. Later in time: after ten o'clock; after lunch

2. Later in a series: Q comes after P in the alphabet.
3. In pursuit of: The dog ran after the cat.

Against

1. In opposition to: Theft is against the law.
2. Touching; supported by: I leaned my bicycle against the wall.

Along

1. Following the length of: We walked along the road.

Among

1. Within a group: The money was shared among three people.

Note: In formal English, among is usually used only when referring to more than two persons or things. In contrast, between is used when referring to two persons or things.

Around

1. Circling something: We walked around the block.
2. Surrounding: There is a fence around the garden.
3. In different parts of: I looked around the house for the keys.
4. In the other direction: We turned around and went back home.
5. Approximately: He is around six feet tall.

At

1. A specific location: at Dominos; at the park
2. A point in time: at 5 o'clock; at Christmas
3. A condition: at peace; at war; at rest
4. An activity: at work; at school; at play

5. Towards: Look at someone; wave at someone

Note: When referring to a specific location or to a point in time, at is usually used. When referring to a certain street or a certain day, on is usually used. When referring to a location as an area, or when referring to a unit of time longer than a day, in is usually used.

E.g. at Christmas; on Christmas day; in the Christmas holidays

Before

1. Earlier in time: before two o'clock; before Christmas
2. Earlier in a series: S comes before T in the alphabet.

Behind

1. At the back of: The little girl hid behind her mother.
2. Late: I am behind in my work.
3. Cause; origin: Who was behind that idea?

Below

1. Lower than; under: below freezing; below sea level.
2. Later on a page: Footnotes are provided below the text.

Beneath

1. Lower than; below: beneath the earth.

Beside

1. Next to; at the side of: I sit beside her in class.

Besides

1. Also; as well as: We study other languages besides English.

Note the differing meanings of beside and besides. Beside is usually used with reference to a physical location.

Between

1. An intermediate location: Delhi lies between Amritsar and Jaipur.
2. An intermediate time: between Christmas and New Year's Day.
3. Intermediate in a series: B comes between A and C in the alphabet.
4. An intermediate amount: between five and ten people.

Beyond

1. Farther than: The mountains lie beyond the horizon.
2. Further than; exceeding: That was beyond my expectations.

But

1. Except: I have read all but the last chapter.

Note: But is used more often as a conjunction than as a preposition.

By

1. Near: a house by the sea.
2. Past: He waved as he drove by the house.
3. Not later than: Try to finish the work by next week.
4. In units of: cheaper by the dozen; sold by weight.
5. Through the means of: travel by plane; written by him.

Note: By is often used in combination with verbs in the Passive Voice.

Concerning

1. Connected with; about: He studies everything concerning trees.

Despite

1. In spite of: We walked downtown despite the rain.

Down

1. To a lower position: The ball rolled down the hill.
2. Further along: He lives down the street.

During

1. Throughout a period: She works during the day.
2. Sometime within a period: An accident occurred during the night.

Except

1. Not including: I have visited everyone except him.

For

1. Duration of time: We walked for two hours.
2. Distance: I walked for five kilometres.
3. Purpose: I bought this jacket for you.
4. In the direction of: She left for Punjabi Bagh.
5. In favour of: We are for the proposal.
6. Considering: The boy is clever for his age.

From

1. Place of origin: We left from Mumbai; he comes from Punjab
2. Start of a period of time: from now on; from yesterday until today
3. Start of a range: From 20 to 30 people were present.
4. Cause: He suffers from nervousness.
5. Source: I first heard the story from you.

In

1. Place thought of as an area: in London; in Europe.
2. Within a location: in the room; in the building.
3. Large units of time: That happened in March, in 1992.
4. Within a certain time: I will return in an hour.
5. By means of: write in pencil; speak in English.
6. Condition: in doubt; in a hurry; in secret.
7. A member of: He is in the orchestra; in the navy.
8. Wearing: the boy in the blue shirt.
9. With reference to: lacking in ideas; rich in oil.

Inside

1. Within: They are inside the house.

Into

1. To the inside of: We stepped into the room.
2. Change of condition: The boy changed into a man.

Like

1. Resembling: That looks like him.
2. Appearing possible: It looks like rain.
3. Be in a suitable mood for: I feel like going swimming.

Minus

1. Less: Three minus two equals one.

Near

1. Close to: near the school; near the ocean.

Of

1. Location: east of here; the middle of the road.

2. Possession: a friend of mine; the sound of music.
3. Part of a group: one of us; a member of the team.

Off

1. Not on; away from: Please keep off the grass.
2. At some distance from: There are islands off the coast.

On

1. Touching the surface of: on the table; on the wall.
2. A certain day: That happened on Sunday, on the 6th of June.
3. A certain street: on South Street.
4. About: a book on engineering.
5. A state or condition: on strike; on fire; on holiday.
6. By means of: live on a pension; shown on television.

Onto

1. To a position on: The child climbed onto the table.

Opposite

1. Facing: The library is opposite the fire station.

Out of

1. To the outside of: She went out of the room.
2. From among: We won two games out of three.
3. Motive: We spoke to them out of politeness.
4. Material: The bridge is made out of steel.
5. Beyond: out of control; out of danger.

Outside

1. On the outer side of: outside the house.
2. Beyond the limits of: outside my experience.

Over

1. Above; higher than: There are cupboards over the sink.
2. Covering: We spread an extra blanket over the bed.
3. Across: I jumped over a puddle.
4. More than: It cost over hundred rupees; it took over an hour.
5. During: I saw him several times over the past week.
6. By means of: We made plans over the telephone.

Past

1. Up to and beyond: I walked past the house.
2. After (in time): It was past 2 o'clock; half past two.
3. Beyond: past belief.

Per

1. For each: 60 kilometres per hour; price per litre

   Plus.

2. With the addition of: Six plus four equals ten.

Since

1. From a specific time in the past: I had been waiting since two o'clock.
2. From a past time until now: I have been waiting here since noon.

Note: Because of its meaning, the preposition since is usually used in combination with a perfect tense. It should be noted that the preposition for can also be used with a perfect tense. However, when used with reference to time, for is usually followed by a phrase referring to a period of time; whereas since is usually followed by a phrase referring to a specific time.

E.g. I have known him for six months.

I have known him since January.

In the first example, for is followed by six months, which refers to a period of time. In the second example, since is followed by January, which refers to a specific time.

Through

1. Across; from end to end of: the main road through town.
2. For the whole of a period: I slept through the night.
3. By means of: Skill improves through practice.

Throughout

1. In every part of: throughout the world.
2. For the whole of a period: throughout the winter.

Till

Note: Till can be used instead of until. However, at the beginning of a sentence, until is usually used.

To

1. In the direction of: Turn to the right.
2. Destination: I am going to Karnataka.
3. Until: from Monday to Friday; five minutes to ten.
4. Compared with: They prefer hockey to soccer.
5. With indirect object: Please give it to me.
6. As part of infinitive: I like to ski; he wants to help.
7. In order to: We went to the store to buy soap.

Toward (or Towards)

1. In the direction of: We walked toward the center of town.
2. Near; just before (time): It rained towards evening.

Under

1. Beneath: under the desk; under the trees.
2. Less than: Under 100 people were present.
3. In circumstances of: under repair; under way; under discussion.

Underneath

1. Below, under: underneath the carpet.

Until

1. Up to a certain time: She will stay until Friday; until 5 p.m.

Upon

Note: On and upon have similar meanings. Upon may be used in certain expressions, as in once upon a time, and following certain verbs, as in to rely upon someone.

Up

1. To a higher place: We went up the stairs.
2. In a higher place: She lives up the hill.

Up to

1. As far as: up to now; I have read up to page 100.
2. Depending on: The decision is up to you.
3. As good as; ready for: His work is up to standard.

Versus

1. Against (sports, legal): The next game is England *versus* Australia.

Via

1. By way of: He went to Panaji via Mumbai.

With

1. Accompanying: He came with her; I have my keys with me.
2. Having; containing: Here is a book with a map of the island.
3. By means of; using: I repaired the shoes with glue.
4. Manner: with pleasure; with ease; with difficulty.
5. Because of: We were paralysed with fear.

Within

1. Inside of: within twenty minutes; within one kilometre

Without

1. Not having: Do not leave without your coat; without money

Prepositions used in Idioms

Below are examples of idioms consisting of prepositional phrases.

At

not at all: not in any way

at all times: always

at any rate: whatever happens

keep someone at arm's length: avoid becoming closely involved with someone

at close quarters: very near

at one's disposal: to be used as one wishes

at a distance: not near

at fault: causing something wrong

at first: at the beginning

see at a glance: see immediately

at hand: near; readily available

at last: finally, after some delay

at a loss: uncertain what to do or say

at the mercy of: without defense against

at the moment: now

at once: immediately

at present: now

at rest: not moving

at risk: threatened by danger or loss

at short notice: with little warning

at stake: to be won or lost

at a stretch: continuously

at that rate: under those circumstances

at this point: at this place; at this moment

Behind

behind the scenes: (of persons) influencing events secretly; (in a theater) behind the stage

behind schedule: not on time

Beside

be beside oneself: lose one's self-control

beside the point: irrelevant

Between

read between the lines: deduce a meaning that is not actually expressed

Beyond

beyond help: unable to be helped

beyond a joke: too annoying to be amusing

beyond reproach: perfect; blameless

By

by accident: not deliberately

by all means: by any possible method

bit by bit: gradually

by chance: by accident; without planning

by courtesy of: with the help or permission of

win by default: win because of lack of competition

by degrees: gradually

perform by ear: perform (music) by listening to the sound, without referring to written music

by hand: without the use of machinery

by heart: from memory

little by little: gradually

by means of: by using

by mistake: accidentally

by no means: not at all

one by one: one at a time

by oneself: alone

side by side: beside one another

by the way: incidentally (used to introduce an unrelated topic of conversation)

by word of mouth: orally

For

once and for all: for the last time (e.g. used when giving someone a final warning)

for certain: definitely; without doubt

for a change: for the sake of variety

for example: as an illustration

for fun: for the sake of enjoyment

for good: permanently

for good measure: in addition to the necessary amount

for instance: for example; as an illustration

for keeps: (colloquial) permanently

for a living: as a profession

for now: temporarily

run for office: compete for an elected position

for one thing: because of one reason (out of several)

for the sake of: for the benefit of; for the purpose of

for sale: intended to be sold

for sure: definitely (more colloquial than for certain)

food for thought: something which makes one think

play for time: delay doing something in the hope that the situation will improve

for the time being: until some other arrangement is made

ask for trouble: act in a dangerous or foolish way

word for word: exactly as said or written

From

from afar: from a distance

from all sides: from all directions

from head to foot: (of a person) completely; all over

from scratch: from the beginning

from time to time: occasionally

In

in addition to: as well as

in advance: before

be in agreement with: have the same opinion as

in any case: whatever happens

in brief: in a few words

in bulk: (of goods) in large amounts; not in packages

be in charge of: have responsibility for

in common: shared by all members of a group

in control: having the power to direct something

in the course of: during

in danger: likely to be harmed

in a daze: unable to think clearly; confused

in debt: owing money

in demand: (of goods or persons) desired by many people

in depth: (investigate something) thoroughly

in detail: (explain something) thoroughly

in disgrace: regarded with disapproval because of having done something wrong

in the distance: far away

in doubt: uncertain

in duplicate: so that there are two identical copies (of a document)

in earnest: seriously; in a determined way

in effect: (of rules) operating

in the end: finally

in fact: in reality; really

in fashion: fashionable; accepted as being the most desirable and up to date

in favour of: supporting (an idea)

in flames: burning, with visible flames

in a flash: very quickly; suddenly

in full: without omitting anything

in general: usually; as a whole

hand in hand: (of persons) holding hands; (of related situations) occurring together

in a hurry: trying to accomplish something quickly

in jest: as a joke

in kind: (payment) in goods rather than in money

in itself: without reference to anything else

in league with: (of persons) joined together with (usually for a dishonest purpose)

be in the limelight: be the focus of attention; receive great publicity

in the long-run: in the end; eventually

in the long-term: looking ahead to the distant future

leave someone in the lurch: abandon someone who is in a difficult situation

be in the minority: be in the smaller of two groups

in mint condition: (of manufactured goods) perfect; brand-new

in a minute: soon

in a moment: soon; quickly

set something in motion: start something going

nip something in the bud: put an end to something before it gets properly started

in no time: very soon; very quickly

in order of: arranged according to

in order to: for the purpose of

in part: to some degree

in particular: especially

in power: (of a political party) holding office

in practice: able to do something well because of recent practice; in reality (opposite of in theory)

in print: (of a book) printed and available from the publisher

in private: not in front of other people

in public: openly; not in private

in reality: really

in reserve: saved for later use

in retrospect: looking back over past events

in return for: as repayment for

be in the right: be correct

in season: (of fruit or vegetables) readily available at that time of year

in a second: soon; quickly

in short supply: scarce; not easily obtainable

in sight: able to be seen

in stock: (of goods at a store) present and available

in that case: if that is true

in theory: ideally; according to theoretical considerations

be in time: not be late

in touch with in: communication with; informed about

in triplicate: so that there are three identical copies (of a document)

be in trouble: be in a difficult situation; be blamed or punished for doing something

Wrong

in tune: at the correct pitch

act in unison: act together

in vain: without success

once in a while: occasionally

in words of one syllable: (explain something) clearly and simply

in working order: able to function properly

in the wrong: responsible for an error; guilty

Inside

inside out: with the inner side out; thoroughly

inside of: within the space or period of/ inner parts or workings

on the inside: inward character, perceptions, or feelings

inside job: arranged or provided by someone within an organisation or building

Into

paint oneself into a corner: take a course of action which greatly narrows one's future choices of action

go into hiding: hide oneself

get into a rut: get into a fixed and uninteresting way of life

get into trouble: get into a difficult situation; do something deserving blame or punishment

Of

of course: certainly; as one would expect; as everyone knows

hard of hearing: somewhat deaf

next of kin: nearest relative or relatives

of one's own accord: voluntarily; on one's own initiative

of one's own free will: voluntarily; by choice

one's point of view: one's opinion about something

right of way: public right to use a path or road; (of road traffic) right to proceed before others

rule of thumb: a simple way to calculate what procedure to

follow, based on extensive experience, rather than on theoretical considerations

Off

go off the air: (of radio or television) stop broadcasting

off duty: not engaged in one's regular work

off one's hands: no longer one's responsibility

off and on: from time-to-time

off the record: say something privately, that is not to be officially recorded

off the track: following a wrong line of thought or action

On

on account of: because of

be on the air: (of radio or television) be in the process of broadcasting

on the alert: ready to act

be on all fours: (of a person) be on hands and knees

on the average: usually; normally

on behalf of: for; in the interests of

on board: on a ship or airplane

on business: as part of one's work

on condition that: only if; provided that

on demand: when asked for

on display: being exhibited

on duty: engaged in one's regular work

on fire: burning

to go on foot: to walk

be on one's guard: be alert and ready to meet an attack

on hand: available

on loan: lent and not yet returned

shoot on location: (of a movie) film in natural surroundings, not in a studio

on the lookout: watchful

put something on the map: cause something to become well-known

get on one's nerves: annoy; irritate

on no account: absolutely not

on the one hand: (used to introduce one side of an argument)

on one's own: alone; without help

act on one's own initiative: act independently, without orders from anyone else

on order: requested but not yet delivered

on the other hand: (used to introduce a contrasting side of an argument)

act on principle: do something to support a policy

on purpose: deliberately

go on record: say something which is to be officially recorded

on sale: being sold at a lower price than usual

on schedule: at the correct time; as planned or predicted

on second thoughts: after thinking further about something

on a shoestring: with a very small amount of money

be on the spot: be where important events are taking place; be placed in an awkward situation

on the spur of the moment: on a sudden impulse

go off on a tangent: change suddenly to a new line of thought or action

on time: at the correct time

walk on tiptoe: walk on the toes and balls of the feet

accept something on trust: accept something without proof

on the verge of: very close to; about to

on the whole: taking everything into consideration

Out of

out of the blue: unexpectedly

out of breath: (after running) panting from a shortage of oxygen

out of character: unlike a person's known character

out of control: not able to be regulated or guided

out of danger: safe

out of date: no longer used; old-fashioned; (of news) no longer true

out of debt: having paid one's debts

be out of one's depth: be unable to handle a situation because of lack of experience

out of doors: in the open air; not in a building

out of fashion: not fashionable; not presently in common use

out of hand: not under control

out of harm's way: safe

out of line with: in disagreement with

be out of one's mind: be insane

out of order: not functioning properly; (at a formal meeting) not behaving according to the rules

out of the ordinary: unusual

out of place: unsuitable

out of practice: unable to do something as well as one has in past, because of lack of recent practice

out of print: (of a book) no longer available from the publisher

out of proportion: too big or too small; not having the appropriate relationship to something out of the question: impossible; not to be considered

out of season: (of fruit or vegetables) not readily available at that time of year

out of shape: (of persons) not in top condition because of lack of exercise

out of sight: hidden, not able to be seen

out of stock: (of goods at a store) temporarily unavailable

out of style: not fashionable

out of touch: with not in communication with; not informed about

out of town: having temporarily left town

out of trouble: not in trouble

out of tune: not at the correct pitch

out of work: no longer having employment

To

to all intents and purposes: in all important ways

to a certain extent: partly

to date: so far; until now

up to date: current; modern

see eye to eye with: agree entirely with

take something to heart: be much affected by something

made to measure: exactly suitable; (of clothes) made for a certain person

keep something to oneself: not tell anyone

to the point: relevant

Under

under age: below the age of being legally permitted to do something

be under arrest: be held prisoner and charged with wrongdoing under the auspices of: with the patronage of; supported by

under one's breath: in a whisper

under the circumstances: because this is true

under consideration: being thought about

under control: able to be regulated or guided

under fire: being shot at; being criticised

under the impression that: having the idea that

be under the influence of: be affected by

be under oath: have sworn to tell the truth

under observation: being watched carefully

under restraint: prevented from doing something

Up

have something up one's sleeve: have a secret idea or plan in reserve

With

with impunity: without risk of injury or punishment

with the naked eye: without using a magnifying lens

with no strings attached: (of help given) with no conditions; to be used freely

take with a pinch of salt: not believe completely

with regard to: concerning; about

with respect to: concerning; about

tarred with the same brush: having the same faults

with a vengeance: very much; more than usual

Within

within limits: to a certain extent; not too much

within living memory: within the memory of people now alive

■■■

CHAPTER 9

Conjunction

A word that is used to join words or phrases or sentences is called a conjunction.

Examples: God made the country and manmade the town.

She must work hard or she will fail.

Madan and Sonu are brothers.

Some facts about Conjunctions:

1. A conjunction is never connected with an object.
2. A conjunction never qualifies a word.

A conjunction is a word that is used for joining two words or groups of words.

Examples: Jaya and Radha are sisters.

He warned me but I did not heed.

Explanation: The word and in the first sentence joins two nouns Jaya and Radha. It is a joining word. But, in the second sentence joins two groups of words: He warned me, I did not heed. It is also a joining word. They are conjunctions.

Note: Conjunctions must be distinguished from relative

pronouns, relative adverbs and prepositions that are also connecting words.

Examples: This is the house that Rahul built. (relative pronoun)

This is the place where he was murdered. (relative adverb)

He sat besides Rama. (preposition)

He stood behind me. (preposition)

Take this and give that. (conjunction)

Explanation: In the above sentences, the relative pronoun refers to the noun house and also joins the two parts of the sentence. The relative adverb modifies the verb was murdered and also joins the two parts of the sentence. The preposition governs the noun or the pronoun while also joining the two words. Whereas, the conjunction merely joins and does no other work.

Some conjunctions are used in pairs.

Examples: Either take it or leave it.

It is neither useful nor ornamental.

We both love and honour him.

Explanation: Either-or, neither-nor, both-and etc. are conjunctions that can be used in pairs and are called correlative conjunctions or correlatives.

When conjunctions are used as correlatives, each of the correlated words should be placed immediately before the words to be connected.

Wrong way: He not only visited Agra, but also Delhi.

Correct way: He visited not only Agra, but also Delhi.

Sometimes compound expressions are used as conjunctions. These are called compound conjunctions.

Examples: The notice was published in order that all might know the facts.

I will forgive you on condition that you do not repeat the offence.

Such an act would not be kind even if it were just.

Kinds of Conjunctions

Coordinating Conjunctions

A coordinating conjunction joins together words or groups of words of equal rank.

Examples: He came to me and asked for alms.

Birds fly and fish swim.

Explanation: The above sentences contain two independent statements of equal rank or importance. Hence the conjunction joining together these two statements of clauses of equal rank is called a coordinating conjunction. And, but, for, or, nor, also, either/or, neither/nor are all examples of coordinating conjunctions.

Coordinating conjunctions are four kinds.

Cumulative or Copulative Conjunction

A cumulative conjunction joins two statements of facts.

Examples: He came to me and asked for alms.

They were both shocked and grieved to hear the news.

He is misled as well as you.

Explanation: In the first sentence the conjunction and joins two statements. He came to me, (he) asked for alms. It is called cumulative conjunction. Similarly both and and in the second sentence, and as well as in the third sentence are cumulative conjunctions.

Adversative Conjunction

Adversative conjunction expresses opposition or contrast between two statements.

Examples: He was rich but not contented.

He was all right; only he was fatigued.

Explanation: In the first sentence the conjunction but shows contrast. It is an adversative conjunction. Similarly in the second sentence only is an adversative conjunction.

Disjunctive or Alternative Conjunction

Disjunctive or alternative conjunction expresses a choice between two alternatives.

Examples: He must participate or he will be fined.

Either you should pay or work for it.

Neither is he hard working nor is he resourceful.

Explanation: Or, either…or, neither….nor are alternative conjunctions because they indicate alternative or choice between two things.

Illative Conjunction

Illative conjunction expresses an inference.

Examples: He will be rewarded, for he is trustworthy.

They are liked, for they are good.

He was guilty; so he was punished.

Explanation: For and so indicate inference or conclusion; so they are illative conjunctions.

Note: Any of the coordinating conjunctions, with the exception of or, nor, may be omitted and its place taken by a comma, semi-colon, or colon.

Example: Rama went out to play: Hari stayed in to work.

Subordinating Conjunctions

A subordinating conjunction joins a clause to another on which it depends for its full meaning.

Examples: I shall help you if you need my help.

I read the paper because it interests me.

Explanation: In the first sentence the conjunction if joins the principal clause and the subordinate clause. It joins two groups of words of unequal rank where one group of words depends on another group of words for its complete meaning. So it is called a subordinating conjunction. Similarly in the second sentence because is a subordinating conjunction. After, because, if, that, though, although, till, before, unless, as, when, where, while etc are all subordinating conjunctions.

Kinds of Subordinating Conjunctions

Subordinating Conjunction of Time

Examples: We went after you left.

It was done before we wanted it.

Explanation: In the examples above after and before illustrate time.

Subordinating Conjunction of Place

Examples: You may go wherever you like.

I searched where I was asked to.

Explanation: In the examples above wherever and where illustrate place.

Subordinating Conjunction of Reason

Examples: I shall do it because I like it.

We did not go out as it was raining.

Explanation: In the examples above because and as illustrate reason.

Subordinating Conjunction of Purpose

Examples: We eat that we may live.

The farmer worked well so that he might get a rich crop.

Explanation: In the examples above that and so that illustrate purpose.

Subordinating Conjunction of Result or Consequence

Examples: It was so clear that all could understand it.

It rained so heavily that all tanks breached.

Explanation: In the examples above that illustrates result or consequence.

Subordinating Conjunction of Condition

Examples: You should do it whether you like it or not.

If you agree I shall accompany you.

Explanation: In the examples above whether and if illustrate condition.

Subordinating Conjunction of Comparison

Examples: She is intelligent as we were told.

You are latter than I.

Explanation: In the examples above as and than illustrate comparison.

Subordinating Conjunction of Concession

Examples: Thought he is ill he has come.

He is strong although he is old.

Explanation: In the examples above though and although illustrate concession.

Parsing of Conjunctions

Parsing model

The boy and his friend are here.

And: Coordinating conjunction, joining the two nouns boy and his friend.

■■■

CHAPTER 10

Interjections

An interjection is a word added to a sentence to convey emotion. It is not grammatically related to any other part of the sentence.

You usually follow an interjection with an exclamation mark. Interjections are uncommon in formal academic prose, except in direct quotations.

Notice the interjections in the following sentences:

Ouch, that hurt!

Oh no, I forgot that the exam was today.

Hey! Put that down!

I heard one guy say to another guy, 'He has a new car, eh?'

I don't know about you but, good lord, I think taxes are too high!

Interjection is a big name for a little word. Interjections are short exclamations like Oh!, Um or Ah! They have no real grammatical value but we use them quite often, usually more in speaking than in writing.

When interjections are inserted into a sentence, they have

no grammatical connection to the sentence. An interjection is sometimes followed by an exclamation mark (!) when written.

Interjections like er and um are also known as 'hesitation devices'. They are extremely common in English. People use them when they don't know what to say, or to indicate that they are thinking about what to say. You should learn to recognize them when you hear them and realise that they have no real meaning.

The table below shows some interjections with examples.

Interjection	Meaning	Example
ah	expressing pleasure	'Ah, that feels good.'
	expressing realization	'Ah, now I understand.'
	expressing resignation	'Ah well, it can't be heped.'
	expressing surprise	'Ah! I've won!'
alas	expressing grief or pity	'Alas, she's dead now.'
dear	expressing pity	'Oh dear! Does it hurt?'
	expressing surprise	'Dear me! That's a surprise!'
eh	asking for repetition	'It's hot today.' 'Eh?' 'I said it's hot today.'
	expressing enquiry	'What do you think of that, eh?'
	expressing surprise	'Eh! Really?'
	inviting agreement	'Let's go, eh?'
er	expressing hesitation	'Lima is the capital of...er...Peru.'
hello, hullo	expressing greeting	'Hello Mamta. How are you today?'
	expressing surprise	'Hello! My car's gone!'
hey	calling attention	'Hey! look at that!'
	expressing surprise, joy etc	'Hey! What a good idea!' hi
expressing greeting	'Hi! What's new?'	
hmm	expressing hesitation, doubt or disagreement	'Hmm. I'm not so sure.'
		Contd..

oh, o	expressing surprise	'Oh! You're here!'
	expressing pain	'Oh! I've got a toothache.'
	expressing pleading	'Oh, please say 'yes'!'
ouch	expressing pain	'Ouch! That hurts!'
uh	expressing hesitation	'Uh...I don't know the answer to that.'
uh-huh	expressing agreement	'Shall we go?' 'Uh-huh.'
um, umm	expressing hesitation	'85 divided by 5 is...um...17.'
well	expressing surprise	'Well I never!'
	introducing a remark	'Well, what did he say?'

Chapter 11

The Tenses

By Tense, we understand the correspondence between the form of the verb and our concept of time.

Tense shows *(a)* the time of an action *(b)* its degree of completeness.

The verb may tell us:

1. That an action is done at the present time, e.g, I see the blue sky.
2. That an action was done in the past time, e.g., He saw the blue sky.
3. That an action was done at some past time, viewed as future(future in the past), e.g. He said that he would be sixteen in three weeks' time.

A verb than, has three main times or tenses, viz., the Present, the Past and the Future.

To each tense, there are four different forms:

Simple which denotes present, past or future time in its simplest form: ' I Play', 'I played', 'I shall play'. The action (in present, past or future time) is mentioned simply, without anything being said about the completeness or incompleteness of the action.

Continuous which denotes that the event (in present, past or future time) is still continuing or not yet completed: ' I am reading', 'I was reading', 'I shall be reading'.

Perfect which denotes that the event (in present, past or future time) is in a completed or perfect state: ' I have played', ' I had played', ' I shall have played'.

Perfect Continuous which combines the meaning of the two preceding forms, ' I have been reading', 'I had been reading' , 'I shall have been reading'.

Present Tense

The Simple Present Tense

The simple present is used to describe an action, an event, or condition that is occurring in the present, at the moment of speaking or writing. The simple present is used when the precise beginning or ending of a present action, event, or condition is unknown or is unimportant to the meaning of the sentence.

Notice the verbs in the following sentences. They are in simple present tense and each sentence describes an action taking place in the present:

Dev waits patiently while Gautam books the tickets.

The shelf holds three books and a vase of flowers.

The crowd moves across the field in an attempt to see the rock star get into her helicopter.

The sisters are both very talented; Vaishali writes and Veena paints.

Rose annoys Varun by turning pages too quickly.

The simple present is used to express general truths such as scientific fact, as in the following sentences:

Rectangles have four sides.

Canada Day takes place on July 1, the anniversary of the signing of the British North America Act.

The Moon circles the Earth once Every 28 days.

Calcium is important to the formation of strong bones.

Menarche and menopause mark the beginning and the ending of a woman's reproductive history.

The simple present is used to indicate a habitual action, event, or condition, as in the following sentences:

My grandmother sends me new mittens each spring.

In fairy tales, things happen in threes.

We never finish jigsaw puzzles because the cat always eats some of the pieces.

The simple present is also used when writing about works of art, as in the following sentences.

Lolly Willowes is the protagonist of the novel Townsend published in 1926.

One of Artemisia Gentleschi's best known paintings represents Judith's beheading of Holofernes.

The Lady of Shallot weaves a tapestry while watching the passers-by in her mirror.

Lear rages against the silence of Cordelia and only belatedly realises that she, not her more vocal sisters, loves him.

The play ends with an epilogue spoken by the fool.

The simple present can also be used to refer to a future event when used in conjunction with an adverb or adverbial phrase, as in the following sentences:

The doors open in 10 minutes.

The premier arrives on Tuesday.

Classes end next week.

The publisher distributes the galley proofs next Wednesday.

The lunar eclipses begins in exactly 43 minutes.

The Present Continuous

While the simple present and the present progressive are sometimes used interchangeably, the present continuous emphasises the continuing nature of an act, event, or condition.

Notice the form of verbs in the following sentences. They are in the present progressive tense. In each sentence the on-going nature of the action is emphasised by the use of the present progressive rather than the simple present.

Nora is looking for the first paperback editions of all of Raymond Chandler's books.

Riya is dusting all the shelves on the second floor of the shop.

The union members are pacing up and down in front of the factory.

KPLA is broadcasting the hits of the 70s this evening.

The presses are printing the first edition of tomorrow's paper.

The present progressive is occasionally used to refer to a future event when used in conjunction with an adverb or adverbial phrase, as in the following sentences.

The boys are coming in 10 minutes.

The flight is arriving on Wednesday.

The dance classes are beginning next week.

The teacher is conducting a quiz next Wednesday.

The Present Perfect Tense

The present perfect tense is used to describe action that began in the past and continues into the present or has just been completed at the moment of utterance. The present perfect is often used to suggest that a past action still has an effect upon something happening in the present.

Notice the compound verbs in the following sentences. They are in the present perfect tense form.

They have not delivered the documents we need.

This sentence suggest that the documents were not delivered in the past and that they are still undelivered.

The health department has decided that all high school students should be immunised against meningitis.

The writer of this sentence uses the present perfect in order to suggest that the decision made in the past is still of importance in the present.

The government has cut university budgets; consequently, the dean has increased the size of most classes.

Here both actions took place sometime in the past and continue to influence the present.

The heat wave has lasted three weeks.

In this sentence, the writer uses the present perfect to indicate that a condition (the heat wave) began in past and continues to affect the present.

Deena has dreamt about frogs sitting in trees every night this week.

Here the action of dreaming has begun in the past and continues into the present.

The Present Perfect Continuous Tense

Like the present perfect, the present perfect continuous is used to describe an action, event, or condition that has begun in the past and continues into the present. The present perfect progressive, however, is used to stress the on-going nature of that action, condition, or event.

Notice the verbs in the following sentences. They are in the present perfect progressive tense and each sentence suggests that the action began in the past and is continuing into the present.

That dog has been barking for three hours; I wonder if someone will call the owner.

I have been relying on my Diwali bonus to pay for the gifts I buy for my large family.

They have been publishing this comic book for ten years.

We have been seeing geese flying south all afternoon.

Even though the coroner has been carefully examining the corpse discovered in cinema hall since early this morning, we still do not know the cause of death.

Past Tense

The Simple Past Tense

The simple past is used to describe an action, an event, or condition that occurred in the past, sometime before the moment of speaking or writing.

Notice the verbs in the following sentences. They are in the simple past tense and each sentence describes an action taking place at some point in past.

A flea jumped from the dog to the cat.

Parul gripped the hammer tightly and nailed the boards together.

The gem-stones sparkled in a velvet lined display case.

Artemisia Gentilsechi probably died in 1652.

The storyteller began every story by saying 'A long time ago when the earth was green.'

The Past Continuous Tense

The past continuous tense is used to described actions ongoing in the past. These actions often take place within a specific time frame. While actions referred to in the present progressive have some connection to the present, actions referred in the past progressive have no immediate or obvious connection to the present. The on-going actions took place and were completed at some point well before the time of speaking or writing.

Notice the verbs in the following sentences. They are in the past progressive tense.

The cat was walking along the tree branch.

This sentence describes an action that took place over a period of continuous time in the past. The cat's actions have no immediate relationship to anything occurring now in the present.

Reena was telling a story about the exploits of a red cow when a tree branch broke the parlour window.

Here the action 'was telling' took place in the past and continued for some time in the past.

When the recess bell rang, Jassy was writing a long division problem on the blackboard.

This sentence describes actions ('ran' and 'was writing') that took place sometime in the past, and emphasises the continuing nature of one of the actions ('was writing').

The archivists were eagerly waiting for the delivery of the former prime minister's private papers.

Here the ongoing action of 'waiting' occurred at some time unconnected to the present.

Between 1942 and 1944 the Frank and Van Damm families were hiding in a Amsterdam office building.

In this sentence, the action of hiding took place over an extended period of time and the continuing nature of the hiding is emphasised.

The Past Perfect Tense

The past perfect tense is used to refer to actions that took place and were completed in the past. The past perfect is often used to emphasise that one action, event or condition ended before another past action, event, or condition began.

Notice the verbs in the following sentences. They are in the past perfect tense.

Monica arrived at 5:00 p.m. but Mr. Talwar had closed the store.

All the events in this sentence took place in the past, but the act of closing the store takes place before Monica arrives at the store.

After we located the restaurant that Christian had raved about, we ate supper there every Friday.

Here the praise ('had raved') precedes the finding ('located') of the restaurant. Both actions took place sometime before the moment of speaking or writing.

The elephant had eaten all the hay so we fed it oats for a week.

In this sentence, both actions take place in the past, but the eating of the hay ('had eaten') preceded the eating of the oats ('fed').

The heat wave had lasted three weeks.

While the sentence 'The heat wave has lasted three weeks' suggests that a condition began in the past and continues into the present, this sentence describes an action that began and ended sometime in the past ('had lasted'). By using the past perfect the writer indicates that the heat wave has no connection to any events occurring in the present.

After she had learned to drive, Alice felt more independent.

Here the learning took place and was completed at a specific time in the past. By using the past perfect rather than the simple past ('learned'), the writer emphasises that the learning preceded the feeling of independence.

The Past Perfect Continuous Tense

The past perfect continuous is used to indicate that a continuing action in the past began before another past action began or interrupted the first action.

Notice the compound verbs in the following sentences. They are in the past perfect progressive tense.

The toddlers had been running around the school yard for ten minutes before the teachers shooed them back inside.

Here the action of the toddlers ('had been running') is ongoing in the past and precedes the actions of the teachers ('shooed') which also takes place in the past.

We had been talking about repainting the front room for three years and last night we finally bought the paint.

In this example, the ongoing action of 'talking' precedes another past action ('bought').

A construction crew had been digging one pit after another in the middle of my street for three days before they found the water main.

Here, the action of digging ('had been digging') took place in the past and occurred over a period of time. The digging was followed by the action of finding ('found').

Geeta had been reading mystery novels for several years before she discovered the works of Agatha Christie.

In this sentence the act of discovery ('discovered') occurred in the past but after the ongoing and repeated action of reading ('had been reading').

The chef's assistant had been chopping vegetables for several minutes before he realised that he had minced his apron strings.

This sentence is a bit more complex in that it contains three different past verb tenses. The sequence of tenses conveys a complex set of information. The past perfect progressive ('had been chopping') is used to emphasise the ongoing nature of the past act of chopping. While a second past perfect progressive ('had been mincing') could be used, the past perfect ('had minced') is used to suggest that act of mincing was completed. The simple past ('realised') is used to describe the action closest to the present, an action that followed both the chopping and the mincing.

Future Tense

The Simple Future Tense

The simple future is used to refer to actions that will take place after the act of speaking or writing.

Notice the verbs in the following sentences. They are in the simple future tense.

They will meet us at the newest café in the market.

Will you walk the dog tonight?

At the feast, we will eat heartily.

Bobby will call you tomorrow with details about the agenda.

The Suresh say that they will not move their chicken coop.

The Future Continuous Tense

The future continuous tense is used to describe actions ongoing in the future. The future progressive is used to refer to continuing action that will occur in the future.

Notice the compound verbs in the following sentences. They are in the future progressive tense.

The glee club will be performing at the celebration of the town's centenary.

Pankaj will be working on the computer system for the next two weeks.

The selection committee will be meeting every Wednesday morning.

We will be writing an exam every afternoon next week.

They will be ringing the bells for Hypatia next month.

The Future Perfect Tense

The future perfect is used to refer to an action that will be completed sometime in the future before another action takes place.

Notice the verbs in the following sentences. They are in the future perfect tense.

The surgeon will have operated on 6 patients before she attends a luncheon meeting.

In this sentence, the act of operating ('will have operated') takes place in the future sometime before the act of attending ('attends').

The plumber and his assistant will have soldered all the new joins in pipes before they leave for the next job.

Here, the plumbers' act of soldering ('will have soldered') will precede the act of leaving ('leave').

By the time you get back from the corner store, we will have finished writing the thank you letters.

In this sentence, the act of returning from the store ('get back') takes place after the act of writing ('will have written').

If this year is like last year, I will have finished my holiday shopping long before my brother starts his.

In this example, the act of finishing ('will have finished') occurs well before the act of starting ('starts').

They will have written their first exam by the time we get out of bed.

Here, the act of getting out of bed occurs sometime after the writing of the exam.

The Future Perfect Continuous Tense

The future perfect progressive tense is used to indicate a continuing action that will be completed at some specified time in the future. This tense is rarely used.

Notice the verbs in the following sentences. They are in the future perfect progressive tense.

I will have been studying French for three years by the end of this term.

In this sentence, the future perfect progressive is used to indicate the ongoing nature of the future act of the studying. The act of studying ('will have been studying') will occur before the upcoming end of term.

By the time the meeting is over, the committee will have been arguing about which candidate to interview for three hours.

Similarly in this sentence, the ongoing nature of a future act ('will have been arguing') is emphasised by the use of the future perfect progressive. The act of sustained arguing will take place before the meeting is over.

When he returns, the wine will have been fermenting for three months.

Here the ongoing action of fermentation will precede ('will have been fermenting') the act of returning.

Verb Tense Overview with Examples

Simple Present	**Simple Past**	**Simple Future**
I study English every day.	Two years ago, I studied English in England.	If you are having problems, I will help you study English. I am going to study English next year.

Present Continuous	Past Continuous	Future Continuous
I am studying English now.	I was studying English when you called yesterday.	I will be studying English when you arrive tonight. I am going to be studying English when you arrive tonight.
Present Perfect	**Past Perfect**	**Future Perfect**
I have studied English in several different countries.	I had studied a little English before I moved to the U.S.	I will have studied every tense by the time I finish this course. I am going to have studied every tense by the time I finish this course.
Present Perfect Continuous	**Past Perfect Continuous**	**Future Perfect Continuous**
I have been studying English for five years.	I had been studying English for five years before I moved to the U.S.	I will have been studying English for over two hours by the time you arrive. I am going to have been studying English for over two hours by the time you arrive.

CHAPTER 12

The Modals

Modals are those helping verbs that express the mode of action denoted by the main verb.

Modals express the mood a verb, such as ability, possibility, necessity, or another condition. They are used with a main verb to form a sentence or a question. Modals are not conjugated, have no tense, and cannot be used without a main verb.

Correct Use of Modals

Serious mistakes are committed in the use of different modals both in speaking as well as writing. It is so because most of us do not know certain facts about modals and do not use them according to the rules of grammar but according to our own convenience. It is, therefore, necessary for us to understand the proper use of modals.

When used with modal verbs (except ought), main verbs always remain in the infinitive without to.

In a statement the word order is subject + modal + main verb.

subject	**modal**	**main verb**
They	can	come.
Rahul	should	walk.

In questions, the word order changes to modal + subject + main verb.

yes-no questions

modal	**subject**	**main verb**
Can	they	come?
Should	Mike	drive?

wh- questions

wh- word	**modal**	**subject**	**main verb**
When	can	they	come?
How	could	he	know?

Can

The modal can indicates possibility or ability:

Tom can help you.

Wild animals can be dangerous.

Dining out can be costly.

In questions, the modal can requests permission to do something or to ask about possibilities:

Can I help you?

Can Mukesh come over for dinner?

Who can answer the next question?

When can we get back the results?

Could

Could indicates possibility or ability in the past:

I could have told you that.

It could have been a disaster.

When I was young, I could run very fast.

Could speculates about future possibilities. In the following examples could and might are synonymous.

It could / might rain tonight.

That could / might be dangerous.

In yes-no questions, could speculates about present possibilities:

Could she be the murderer?

Could this be a mistake?

It can also make a request. In these examples could and can are synonymous, but could is more polite.

Could / Can you open your window?

Could / Can you help me move this sofa?

Could indicates an option:

We could go see a movie.

I could become a doctor.

The modal could is also used to form the conditional. The conditional contains an if clause and a result clause. Could is placed in the result clause.

In these examples, could expresses hypothetical situations:

If I had time, I could play tennis with you.

We could study together, if you want to.

If it weren't raining, we could go on a picnic.

Could mentions something that didn't happen because a certain condition was not met:

If we had left sooner, we could have taken the train.

I could have passed the exam if I had studied more.

I'm glad we took umbrellas. We could have gotten soaked.

Shall and Will

The modals shall/will + main verb are used to create future tenses. These modals indicate an intention or an action that is expected to happen in the future.

When used in statements, there is no difference in meaning between these two modals; however, shall is rarely used in American English.

I will / shall close the door for you.

Tom will / shall meet us at the train station.

They will / shall leave tomorrow at 8:00.

In wh- questions, shall and will ask about options.

Who will / shall drive the car?

When will / shall I see you again?

How will / shall you get here?

What time will / shall we meet?

In yes-no questions, shall and will have different meanings.

Will asks a favour.

Will / Shall you turn off the TV?

Will / Shall you stop whining?

Will / Shall you go with me?

Will also asks for information or knowledge about somebody or something.

Will / Shall Tom ever pay you back?

Will / Shall Mars be visited by humans within twenty years?

Will / Shall you be finished soon?

Shall asks about a preference. In these examples, shall and should are synonymous. In American English, shall is rarely used; when it is, it's only in the first person singular and plural.

Should / Shall I close the door?

Should / Shall he close the door?

Should / Shall they come back later?

Should / Shall Tittoo bring food to the party?

Should / Shall we stay here?

May and Might

The modals may and might indicate an uncertain future action. These two modals are synonymous.

I may / might go to the park, or I may / might stay home.

This may / might be a bad idea.

It may / might rain tonight.

May or can gives instructions or permission.

You may / can now board the airplane.

You may / can begin the exam in ten minutes.

In yes-no questions that make a request, you can use may or can. May is more polite.

May / Can I see your driver's license?

May / Can we have some more water, please?

You can might in place of may or can, but this is extremely rare in American English.

May / Can / Might I be of some assistance?

May / Can / Might we offer you a suggestion?

Must

The modal must indicates an obligation.

You must see this movie.

Tarun must see a doctor immediately.

Must also indicates an assumption or probability.

My watch must be broken.

He must have done that before moving to Mumbai.

In wh- questions, must is an obligation and can be replaced with the modal should. In American English, should is much more common in these types of questions.

When should / must we be there?

Who should / must I talk to?

Must can sometimes form rhetorical questions, when you want the person to stop doing something.

Must you make so much noise?	=	Please be quiet.
Must he ask so many questions?	=	I hope he stops asking questions.

Should and Ought (to)

The modals should and ought to indicate an obligation. These two modals are synonymous.

You should / ought to call your mother.

I should / ought to go home now.

When used in questions, should asks if an obligation exists. Ought is never used in questions in American English.

Should he call her?

Should we pay now?

When should we leave?

What should I wear?

Would

Would followed by like is a polite way of stating a preference.

I would like white wine with my fish.

We would like a room with a view.

In questions, would + subject + like is a polite request for a choice to be made.

Would you like soup or salad with your meal?

Where would you like to eat dinner?

When would Tom like this delivered?

Would can make a request sound more polite.

Come here!	Would you come here?
Stop making that noise!	Would you stop making that noise?

Would explains an action as a result of a supposed or real condition.

I would go with you if I didn't have to work.

If I had not had to work, I would have gone with you.

She would be surprised if you came to the party.

Rahul would drive, but he doesn't have a license.

Would introduces habitual actions in the past.

When I was a student, I would go swimming every day.

When Rahul lived in USA, he would write me long letters.

Note:

1.	Do not use modals for things which happen definitely.	The sun rises in the East.
2.	They do not have an -s in the 3rd person singular.	He can play football.
3.	Questions are formed without do/does/did.	Can he speak Spanish?
4.	It follows a full verb in the infinitive.	They must read the book.
5.	There are no past forms (except could and would).	He was allowed to watch the film.
6.	When you use the past participle, you tell about things which did not happen in the past.	You should have told me.

Form

Positive		Negative	
long form	**contracted form**	**long form**	**contracted form**
can	—	cannot	can't
could	—	could not	couldn't
may	—	may not	—
might	—	might not	—
ought to	—	ought not to	oughtn't to
—	—	need not	needn't
shall	'll	shall not	shan't
should	'd	—	shouldn't
will	'll	will not	won't
would	'd	would not	wouldn't

Use of Modals with Example

Modal	Example	Uses
Can	They can control their own budgets.	Ability / Possibility
	We can't fix it.	Inability / Impossibility
	Can I smoke here?	Asking for permission
	Can you help me?	Request
Could	Could I borrow your dictionary?	Asking for permission.
	Could you say it again more slowly?	Request
	We could try to fix it ourselves.	Suggestion
	I think we could have another Gulf War.	Future possibility
	He gave up his old job so he could work for us.	Ability in the past
May	May I have another cup of coffee?	Asking for permission
	China may become a major economic power.	Future possibility
Might	We'd better phone tomorrow, they might be eating their dinner now.	Present possibility
	They might give us a 10% discount.	Future possibility
Must	We must say good-bye now.	Necessity / Obligation

Contd...

	They mustn't disrupt the work more than necessary.	Prohibition
Ought to	We ought to employ a professional writer.	Saying what's right or correct
Shall	Shall I help you with your luggage?	Offer
(More common in the UK	Shall we say 2.30 then?	Suggestion
than the US)	Shall I do that or will you?	Asking what to do
Should	We should sort out this problem at once.	Saying what's right or correct
	I think we should check everything again.	Recommending action
	Profits should increase next year.	Uncertain prediction
Will	I can't see any taxis so I'll walk.	Instant decisions
	I'll do that for you if you like.	Offer
	I'll get back to you first thing on Monday.	Promise
	Profits will increase next year.	Certain prediction
Would	Would you mind if I brought a colleague with me?	Asking for permission
	Would you pass the salt please?	Request
	Would you mind waiting a moment?	Request
	'Would three o'clock suit you?' - 'That'd be fine.'	Making arrangements
	Would you like to play golf this Friday?	Invitation
	'Would you prefer tea or coffee?' - 'I'd like tea please.'	Preferences

CHAPTER 13

The Articles

Articles play a very important role in ensuring that we speak and write correct English. A wrong use of articles can sometimes lead to a change in the meaning of the word altogether. Use of some articles depends strictly on the sound produced by them. They are also called Determiners.

English has two articles: the and a/an. The is used to refer to specific or particular nouns; a/an is used to modify non-specific or non-particular nouns. We call the definite article and a/an the indefinite article.

the = definite article

a/an = indefinite article

For example, if I say, 'Let's read the book,' I mean a specific book. If I say, 'Let's read a book,' I mean any book rather than a specific book.

Here's another way to explain it: The is used to refer to a specific or particular member of a group. For example, 'I just saw the most popular movie of the year.' There are many movies, but only one particular movie is the most popular. Therefore, we use the.

'A/an' is used to refer to a non-specific or non-particular member of the group. For example, 'I would like to go see a movie.' Here, we're not talking about a specific movie. We're talking about any movie. There are many movies, and I want to see any movie. I don't have a specific one in mind.

Let's look at each kind of article a little more closely.

Indefinite Articles: a and an

'A' and 'an' signal that the noun modified is indefinite, referring to any member of a group. For example:

'My daughter really wants a dog for Diwali.' This refers to any dog. We don't know which dog because we haven't found the dog yet.

'Somebody call a policeman!' This refers to any policeman. We don't need a specific policeman; we need any policeman who is available.

'When I was at the zoo, I saw an elephant!' Here, we're talking about a single, non-specific thing, in this case an elephant. There are probably several elephants at the zoo, but there's only one we're talking about here.

Remember, using a or an depends on the sound that begins the next word. So...

a + singular noun beginning with a consonant: a boy; a car; a bike; a zoo; a dog

an + singular noun beginning with a vowel: an elephant; an egg; an apple; an idiot; an orphan

a – singular noun beginning with a consonant sound: a user (sounds like 'yoo-zer,' i.e. begins with a consonant 'y' sound, so 'a' is used); a university; a unicycle

an + nouns starting with silent 'h': an hour

In some cases where 'h' is pronounced, such as 'historical,' use an:

An historical event is worth recording.

In writing, 'a historical event' is more commonly used.

Remember that this rule also applies when you use acronyms:

Introductory Composition at Purdue (ICaP) handles first-year writing at the University. Therefore, an ICaP memo generally discusses issues concerning English 106 instructors.

Another case where this rule applies is when acronyms start with consonant letters but have vowel sounds:

An MSDS (material safety data sheet) was used to record the data. An SPCC plan (Spill Prevention Control and Countermeasures plan) will help us prepare for the worst.

If the noun is modified by an adjective, the choice between a and an depends on the initial sound of the adjective that immediately follows the article:

a broken egg

an unusual problem

a European country (sounds like 'yer-o-pi-an,' i.e. begins with consonant 'y' sound)

Remember, too, that in English, the indefinite articles are used to indicate membership in a group:

I am a teacher. (I am a member of a large group known as teachers.)

Brian is an Irishman. (Brian is a member of the people known as Irish.)

Seiko is a practicing Buddhist. (Seiko is a member of the group of people known as Buddhists.)

Definite Article: the

The definite article is used before singular and plural nouns when the noun is specific or particular. The signals that the noun is definite, that it refers to a particular member of a group. For example:

'The dog that bite me ran away.' Here, we're talking about a specific dog, the dog that bite me.

'I was happy to see the policeman who saved my cat!' Here, we're talking about a particular policeman. Even if we don't know the policeman's name, it's still a particular policeman because it is the one who saved the cat.

'I saw the elephant at the zoo.' Here, we're talking about a specific noun. Probably there is only one elephant at the zoo.

Count and Noncount Nouns

The can be used with noncount nouns, or the article can be omitted entirely.

'I love to sail over the water' (some specific body of water) or 'I love to sail over water' (any water).

'He spilled the milk all over the floor' (some specific milk, perhaps the milk you bought earlier that day) or 'He spilled milk all over the floor' (any milk).

'A/an' can be used only with count nouns.

'I need a bottle of water.'

'I need a new glass of milk.'

Most of the time, you can't say, 'She wants a water,' unless you're implying, say, a bottle of water.

Geographical use of 'the'

There are some specific rules for using 'the' with geographical nouns.

Do not use 'the' before:

names of most countries/territories: Italy, Mexico, Bolivia;

however, the Netherlands, the Dominican Republic, the Philippines, the United States

names of cities, towns, or states: Seoul, Manitoba, Mumbai

names of streets: M.G. Road, Park Street.

names of lakes and bays: Lake Titicaca, Lake Erie except with a group of lakes like the Great Lakes

names of mountains: Mount Everest, Mount Fuji except with ranges of mountains like the Andes or the Rockies or unusual names like the Matterhorn

names of continents (Asia, Europe)

names of islands (Easter Island, Maui, Key West) except with island chains like the Aleutians, the Hebrides, or the Canary Islands.

Do use 'the' before:

names of rivers, oceans and seas: the Nile, the Pacific, the Gangas.

points on the globe: the Equator, the North Pole

geographical areas: the Middle East, the West

deserts, forests, gulfs, and peninsulas: the Sahara, the Persian Gulf, the Black Forest, the Iberian Peninsula

Omission of Articles

Some common types of nouns that don't take an article are:

Names of languages and nationalities: French, Chinese, English, Spanish, Russian (unless you are referring to the population of the nation: 'The Spanish are known for their warm hospitality.')

Names of sports: volleyball, hockey, baseball, cricket

Names of academic subjects: mathematics, biology, history, computer science

■■■

CHAPTER 14

Voice (Active and Passive)

Voice is that branch of grammar which studies the form that the verb takes in a sentence to determine the status of the subject and the object.

Voice can be studied under the following headings:

1. **Active voice**: A verb is said to be in the active voice when its subject acts or when the emphasis is on the doer or the subject. The active voice is so called because the person or thing denoted by the subject acts.

   Example: Mohan sang a song.

   Here, the Subject Mohan is acting.

2. **Passive Voice:** A verb is in the passive voice when the subject is being acted upon or when the emphasis is on the objector the work done. The passive voice is so called because the person or thing denoted by the subject that is not active but passive, and receives some action.

   Example:A song was sung by Mohan.

   Here, the subject is being acted upon.

   Note: Voice changes occur only in transitive verbs.

The perfect continuous form of all the three tenses and future continuous cannot be changed into passive voice.

Sentences can be active or passive. Therefore, tenses also have 'active forms' and 'passive forms.' You must learn to recognise the difference to successfully speak English.

Active Form

In active sentences, the thing doing the action is the subject of the sentence and the thing receiving the action is the object. Most sentences are active.

[Thing doing action] + [verb] + [thing receiving action]

Examples:

The professor	teaches	the students.
subject doing action	verb	object receiving action
Jatin	washes	the dishes
subject doing action	verb	object receiving action

Passive Form

In passive sentences, the thing receiving the action is the subject of the sentence and the thing doing the action is optionally included near the end of the sentence. You can use the passive form if you think that the thing receiving the action is more important or should be emphasised. You can also use the passive form if you do not know who is doing the action or if you do not want to mention who is doing the action.

[Thing receiving action] + [be] + [past participle of verb] + [by] + [thing doing action]

Examples:

The students	are taught	by the professor.
subject receiving action	passive verb	doing action
The dishes	are washed	by Jatin
subject receiving action	passive verb	doing action

How to change Active Voice into Passive Voice

1. In an Active Voice the form of verb shows that the person denoted by the subject in the sentence does something.

   Examples: (i) Amit reads a book

   (ii) Rohit writes a letter

Amit and Rohit are the doers of action in sentence *(i)* and *(ii)*

In Passive Voice the form of verb shows that something is done to the person denoted by the subject.

   Examples: (i) A book is read by Amit.

   (ii) A letter written by Rohit.

In sentence *(i)* action is done to the book and in sentence *(ii)* the action is done to the letter.

Thus the VOICE is that form of a verb which shows whether what is denoted by the subject does something or has something done to it.

2. While changing the Active Voice to Passive Voice , we change the object of the Active Voice into the subject of the Passive Voice.

   Examples: (i) Ram Loves Shyam (Active)

   (ii) Shyam is loved by Ram (Passive)

Ram the subject of sentence *(i)* change into the object in sentence *(ii)*

3. Only Sentences having transitive verbs can be changed into Passive Voice because the intransitive verbs do not have Subject.

4. In Simple Present Tense in Active Voice the Ist form of the Verb+s/es is used and when we convert these kind of sentences into Passive Voice the third form of the verb is used with the helping verbs like is, am, are according to the subject.

Examples: Mother cooks the food. (Active)

The food is cooked by mother. (Passive)

The same rule is applied for the past continuous tense here we use 2nd form of the verb in Active but in Passive voice we use was and were with the 3rd form of Verb.

Examples: She took her breakfast. (Active)

Her breakfast was taken by her. (Passive)

In Simple future we use will/shall and the Ist form of verb in Active Voice but in Passive voice we use will be/shall be with the 3rd form of verb.

Examples: I shall write a letter.

A letter shall be written by me.

5. In Present Continuous Tense in Active Voice the Ist form of the Verb+ing is used and when we convert these kind of sentences into Passive Voice the third form of the verb is used with the being.

Examples: I am singing a song (Active)

A song is being sung by me. (Passive)

The same rule is applied for the past continuous tense here we use was and were as a helping verb instead of is, am, are.

Example: I was singing a song (Active)

A song was being sung by me. (Passive)

Future Continuous tense do not have any Passive.

6. In Present Perfect Tense in Active Voice the has/have and the 3rd form of the Verb is used and when we convert these kind of sentences into Passive Voice the third form of the verb is used with has been/have been instead has/have.

Examples: He has divulged the secret.(Active)

The secret has been divulged by him. (Passive)

The same rule is applied for the past perfect tense here we use had as a helping verb instead of has/have.

Examples: They had arranged the meeting.(Active)

The meeting had been arranged by them. (Passive)

The same rule is applied for the future perfect tense here we use shall/will have as a helping verb instead of has/have.

Examples: You will have obtained admission.(Active)

Admission will have been obtained by you. (Passive)

7. Change of persons as Subjects-Objects

I	my	me
We	our	us
You	your	you
He	his	him
she	her	her
They	their	them

In English grammar, voice shows whether the subject of a sentence is doing the action, or having the action done to it.

The Active Voice

We say things in the active voice when we want to show who or what has done something. In the active voice the agent (the person or thing that does something) becomes the subject of the sentence.

Examples: 'She cleaned the office.' (Who cleaned the office? She did=the subject)

'He stole my car.' (Who stole my car? He did=the subject)

The active voice uses fewer words than the pompous

sounding passive voice. Some tests often include passive constructions that need revision.

The Passive Voice

The passive voice may use any tense of the verb to be:-

	to be		**past participle**
I / It / They etc.	is / are / am	(present simple)	finished.
	was / were	(past simple)	
I / It / They etc.	is being / are being / am being	(present continuous)	
	was being / were being	(past continuous)	cleaned.
I / It / They etc.	has been / have been	(present perfect)	sent.
	had been	(past perfect)	
I / It / They etc.	will be	(future)	tired.

The passive voice is used when the subject of a sentence is the person or thing affected by the action of the sentence.

We particularly use the passive voice when we don't know or aren't bothered exactly who has done something. This is called passive without agent where the recipient of the action becomes the subject.

Example: 'The office was cleaned.' (What was cleaned? - The office=the subject)

We often use the passive to report what someone has said but we want to avoid telling anyone who said it.

Example: 'I was told you weren't coming.'

Sometimes it is used in order to deliberately avoid saying who did something, or more often who's to blame for something. Either because you don't know, or because you don't want to say. You'll often see it used in politics, the business world, or in any other activity involving bureaucracy.

'The civilian was shot.' (Who was shot? The civilian=the subject)

'The report was mislaid.' (What was mislaid? The report =the subject)

Sometimes you may want to use the passive voice but wish to mention who carried out the action. This is called passive with agent and the agent is usually introduced with the word by.

Example: 'The office was cleaned by Mrs Shiela.'

Or you may use a subject such as people, someone, they etc, when you don't know who the agent is.

Example: 'The car was stolen by joy riders.'

When you can't use the passive

Intransitive verbs cannot be used in the passive. This is because they cannot have objects, and so there is nothing to become the subject of the passive sentence. For example with verbs like die or arrive.

Active and Passive Tenses Chart

SIMPLE PRESENT and SIMPLE PAST

The active object becomes the passive subject.

am/is/are + past participle

was/were + past participle

Active: Simple Present	**Passive: Simple Present**
The movie fascinates me.	I am fascinated by the movie.
The movie bores Jack.	Jack is bored by the movie.
The movie surprises them.	They are surprised by the movie.
Active: Simple Past	**Passive: Simple Past**
The movie bored me.	I was bored by the movie.
The movie fascinated Jack.	Jack was fascinated by the movie.
The movie surprised them.	They were surprised by the movie.

PRESENT and PAST CONTINUOUS (PROGRESSIVE)

Passive form:

am/is/are + being + past participle

was/were + being + past participle

Active: Present Continuous	Passive: Present Continuous
I am helping Sarita.	Sarita is being helped by me.
Priya is helping Meena and Leena.	Meena and Leena are being helped by Priya.
Active: Past Continuous	**Passive: Past Continuous**
I was cleaning the bathroom.	The bathroom was being cleaned by me.
They were cleaning the bedroom.	The bedroom was being cleaned by them.
Susan was cleaning the kitchen and patio.	The kitchen and patio were being cleaned by Susan.

PRESENT PERFECT, PAST PERFECT and FUTURE PERFECT

Passive form:

have/has been + past participle

had been + past participle

Active: Present Perfect	Passive: Present Perfect
I have mailed the gift.	The gift has been mailed by me.
Rahul has mailed the gifts.	The gifts have been mailed by Rahul.
Active: Past Perfect	**Passive: Past Perfect**
Steven Spielberg had directed the movie.	The movie had been directed by Steven Spielberg.
Penny Marshall had directed those movies.	The movies had been directed by Penny Marshall.
Active: Future Perfect	**Passive: Future Perfect**
Gaurav will have finished the project next month.	The project will have been finished by next month by Gaurav.
They will have finished the projects before then.	The projects will have been finished before then.

FUTURE TENSES

Passive forms: will + be + past participle

is/are going to be + past participle

Active: Future with WILL	Passive: Future with WILL
I will mail the gift.	The gift will be mailed by me.
Jatin will mail the gifts.	The gifts will be mailed by Jatin.

Active: Future with GOING TO	**Passive: Future with GOING TO**
I am going to make the cake.	The cake is going to be made by me.
Sarita is going to make two cakes.	Two cakes are going to be made by Sarita.

PRESENT / FUTURE MODALS

The passive form follows this pattern:

modal + be + past participle

Active: WILL / WON'T (WILL NOT)	**Passive: WILL / WON'T (WILL NOT)**
Sharon will invite Tarun to the party.	Tarun will be invited to the party by Sharon.
Sharon won't invite Hari to the party.	Hari won't be invited to the party by Sharon.
(Sharon will not invite Hari to the party.)	(Hari will not be invited to the party by Sharon.)
Active: CAN / CAN'T (CAN NOT)	**Passive: CAN / CAN'T (CAN NOT)**
Geeta can foretell the future.	The future can be foretold by Geeta.
Sunita can't foretell the future.	The future can't be foretold by Sunita.
(Sunita cannot foretell the future.)	(The future can not be foretold by Sunita.)
Active: MAY / MAY NOT	**Passive: MAY / MAY NOT**
Her company may give Katya a new office.	Katya may be given a new office by her company.
The lazy students may not do the homework.	The homework may not be done by the lazy students.
MIGHT / MIGHT NOT	**MIGHT / MIGHT NOT**
Her company might give Katya a new office.	Katya might be given a new office by her company.
The lazy students might not do the homework.	The homework might not be done by the lazy students.
Active: SHOULD / SHOULDN'T	**Passive: SHOULD / SHOULDN'T**
Students should memorise English verbs.	English verbs should be memorised by students.
Children shouldn't smoke cigarettes.	Cigarettes shouldn't be smoked by children.
Active: OUGHT TO	**Passive: OUGHT TO**
Students ought to learn English verbs. (negative ought to is rarely used)	English verbs ought to be memorised by students.

Active: HAD BETTER / HAD BETTER NOT	Passive: HAD BETTER / HAD BETTER NOT
Students had better practice English every day.	English had better be practiced every day by students.
Children had better not drink whiskey.	Whiskey had better not be drunk by children.
Active: MUST / MUST NOT	**Passive: MUST / MUST NOT**
Tourists must apply for a passport to travel abroad.	A passport to travel abroad must be applied for.
Customers must not use that door.	That door must not be used by customers.
Active: HAS TO / HAVE TO	**Passive: HAS TO / HAVE TO**
She has to practice English every day.	English has to be practiced every day.
Sara and Miho have to wash the dishes every day.	The dishes have to be washed by them every day.
DOESN'T HAVE TO/ DON'T HAVE TO	**DOESN'T HAVE TO/ DON'T HAVE TO**
Maria doesn't have to clean her bedroom every day.	Her bedroom doesn't have to be cleaned every day.
The children don't have to clean their bedrooms every day.	Their bedrooms don't have to be cleaned every day.
Active: BE SUPPOSED TO	**Passive: BE SUPPOSED TO**
I am supposed to type the composition.	The composition is supposed to be typed by me.
I am not supposed to copy the stories in the book.	The stories in the book are not supposed to be copied.
Janet is supposed to clean the living room.	The living room is supposed to be cleaned by Janet.
She isn't supposed to eat candy and gum.	Candy and gum aren't supposed to be eaten by her.
They are supposed to make dinner for the family.	Dinner for the family is supposed to be made by them.
They aren't supposed to make dessert.	Dessert isn't supposed to be made by them.

PAST MODALS

The past passive form follows this pattern:

modal + have been + past participle

Active: SHOULD HAVE / SHOULDN'T HAVE	**Passive: SHOULD HAVE / SHOULDN'T HAVE**
The students should have learned the verbs.	The verbs should have been learned by the students.
The children shouldn't have broken the window.	The window shouldn't have been broken by the children.
Active: OUGHT TO	**Passive: OUGHT TO**
Students ought to have learned the verbs.	The verbs ought to have been learned by the students.
(negative ought to is rarely used)	
Active: BE SUPPOSED TO (past time)	**Passive: BE SUPPOSED TO (past time)**
I was supposed to type the composition.	The composition was supposed to be typed by me.
I wasn't supposed to copy the story in the book.	The story in the book wasn't supposed to be copied.
Janet was supposed to clean the living room.	The living room was supposed to be cleaned by Janet.
She wasn't supposed to eat candy and gum.	Candy and gum weren't supposed to be eaten by her.
Frank and Jane were supposed to make dinner.	Dinner was supposed to be made by them.
They weren't supposed to make dessert.	Dessert wasn't supposed to be made by them.
Active: MAY / MAY NOT	**Passive: MAY / MAY NOT**
That firm may have offered Katya a new job.	Katya may have been offered a new job by that firm.
The students may not have written the paper.	The paper may not have been written by the students.
MIGHT / MIGHT NOT	**MIGHT / MIGHT NOT**
That firm might have offered Katya a new job.	Katya might have been offered a new job by that firm.
The students might not have written the paper.	The paper might not have been written by the students.

■■■

Chapter 15

Narration

In our speech, we often speak to the other person of some thing that was said to us by somebody. In other words, we often report a speech whether ours or someone else's. We do this in two ways. We either report the speech exactly as we had heard or said it without making any change. This is called Direct Speech.

Example: The girl said to her mother, 'My plate is empty.'

Or we may change the sentence that we had heard or said without changing its meaning and then report it. This is called Indirect speech.

Example: The girl said to her mother that her plate was empty.

In the first example, the first part of the sentence which is before the comma, is referred to as reporting verb and the part which is within inverted commas is called the reported speech.

Note: While transforming from direct into indirect, we have made several changes in the sentence above:

1. We have removed the comma in the indirect sentence and put that in its place.

2. We have removed the inverted commas of the reported speech.
3. We have changed the my of the reported speech into her.
4. We have not used any capital in between the sentence unlike in the direct from where the reported speech always begins with a capital letter.

Now, in order to bring about these changes while converting from direct into indirect or vice versa, there are several important but simple rules that need to be observed.

In this section, We are going to see How the conversion of Direct to Indirect Speech and Indirect to Direct Speech is done?

We may report the words of a speaker in two ways:

1. Direct Speech: We may quote the actual words of the speaker. This method is called Direct Speech.
2. Indirect Speech: We may report what he said without quoting his exact words. This method is called Indirect Speech or Reported Speech.

Example:

- Direct: Clinton said, 'I am very busy now.'
- Indirect: Clinton said that he was very busy then.
- Direct : He said, ' my mother is writing letter.'
- Indirect: He said that his mother was writing letter.

How to Change Direct to Indirect Speech?

It will be noticed that in Direct Speech, we use inverted commas to mark off the exact words of the speaker. In Indirect Speech we do not use the inverted commas.

It will be further noticed that in changing the above Direct Speech into Indirect speech, certain changes have been made.

Thus:

(i) We have used the conjunction 'that' before the Indirect Statement.

(ii) The pronoun 'I' is changed to 'HE'. (The Pronoun is changed in Person)

(iii) The verb 'am' is changed to 'was'.

(iv) The adverb 'now' is changed to 'then'.

Rules for changing Direct into Indirect Speech:

A. When the reporting or principal verb is in the Past Tense, all the Present Tenses in the Direct Speech are changed into Past Tense.

(a) A simple present tense becomes simple past tense.

Example:

- Direct : He said, 'I am unwell.'
- Indirect: He said that he was unwell.

(b) A present continuous tense becomes a past continuous.

Example:

- Direct : He said, ' my mother is writing letter.'
- Indirect: He said that his mother was writing letter.

(c) A present perfect becomes a past perfect:

Are you clear about the conversion of Direct to Indirect Speech?

Example:

- Direct: He said, 'I have passed the examination.'
- Indirect: he said that he had passed the examination.

(d) As a rule the simple past tense in the Direct Speech becomes the past perfect tense in Indirect Speech.

Example:

- Direct: He said, 'His horse died in the night.'
- Indirect: he said that his horse had died in the night.

Note: The shall of the future is changed into should.

The will of the future is changed into would.

The can and may of the future are changed into could and might respectively.

Are you clear about the conversion of Direct to Indirect Speech?

B. The tenses will not change if the statement is still relevant or if it is a universal truth. We can often choose whether to keep The original tenses or change them.

Examples:

- Direct: 'I know her address', said Rahul.
- Indirect: Rahul said that he knows/knew her address.

In this Indirect Speech, both the past tense and the present tense make the sentence a correct one.

- Direct: The teacher said, 'The earth goes round the sun.'
- Indirect: The teacher said that the earth goes/went round the sun.
- Direct: She said, 'German is easy to learn.'
- Indirect: She said that German was/is easy to learn.

The past tense is often used when it is uncertain if the statement is true or when we are reporting objectively.

Are you clear about the conversion of Direct to Indirect Speech?

C. If the reporting verb is in present tense, the tenses of the Direct Speech do not change. For example, we may rewrite the above examples, putting the reporting verb in the present tense.

Examples:

- Direct : He says, 'I am unwell.'
- Indirect: He says that he is unwell.
- Direct : He says, ' my mother is writing letter.'
- Indirect: He says that his mother is writing letter.
- Direct: He says, 'I have passed the examination.'
- Indirect: he says that he has passed the examination.
- Direct: He says, 'His horse died in the night.'
- Indirect: he says that his horse died in the night.

Are you clear about the conversion of Direct to Indirect Speech?

D. The pronouns of the Direct Speech are changed where necessary, so that their relations with the reporter and his hearer, Rather than with the original speaker are indicated.

Examples:

- Direct: He said to me, 'I do not believe you.'
- Indirect: He said that he did not believe me.
- Direct: She said to him, 'I do not believe you.'
- Indirect: She said to him that she did not believe him.
- Direct: I said to him, 'I did not believe you.'
- Indirect: I said to him that I did not believe him.
- Direct: I said to you, 'I do not believe you.'
- Indirect: I said to you that I do not believe you.

Are you clear about the conversion of Direct to Indirect Speech?

E. Words expressing nearness in time or places are generally changed into words expressing distance.

Examples:

- Direct: He said, 'I am glad to be here this evening.'
- Indirect: he said that he was glad to be there that evening.
- Direct: He said, 'I was here yesterday.'
- Indirect: He said that he was there the day before.

Are you clear about the conversion of Direct to Indirect Speech?

Now, let us see the words which get changed when the Direct Speech is changed into Indirect Speech.

- Now becomes then
- Here becomes there
- Ago becomes before
- Thus becomes so
- Today becomes that day
- Tomorrow becomes the next day
- Yesterday becomes the day before
- Last night becomes the night before
- This becomes that
- These becomes those

Are you clear about the conversion of Direct to Indirect Speech?

F. How the questions used in the Direct Speech are changed into Indirect Speech?

In reporting questions, the indirect Speech is introduced by such verbs as asked, inquired etc...

Examples:

- Direct: He said to me, 'What are you doing?'
- Indirect: He asked me what I was doing.

- Direct: A stranger asked me, 'Where do you live?'
- Indirect: A stranger enquired where I lived.
- Direct: The Policemen said to us, 'Where are you going?'
- Indirect: The Policemen asked us where we were going.
- Direct: He said, 'Will you listen to such a man?'
- Indirect: He asked them whether they would listen to such a man.
- Indirect: Would they, he asked, listen to such a man.
- Direct: His angry mother jeered, 'Do you suppose you know better than your father?'
- Indirect: His angry mother jeered and asked whether he supposed that he knew better than his father.

Are you clear about the conversion of Direct to Indirect Speech?

G. How the Commands and the Requests in the Direct Speeches are changed when the Direct Speeches are changed into indirect Speeches?

In reporting commands and requests, the indirect speech is introduced by some verb expressing commands and requests, and the Imperative Mood is changed into Infinitive Mood.

Examples:

- Direct: Raja said to Rahul, 'Go away.'
- Indirect: Raja ordered Rahul to go away.
- Direct: He said to Manisha, 'Please wait here till I return.'
- Indirect: he requested Manisha to wait there till he returned.

Are you clear about the conversion of Direct to Indirect Speech?

- Direct: 'Call the first witness', said the Judge.

- Indirect: The Judge commanded them to call the first witness.
- Direct: He shouted, 'Let me go.'
- Indirect: he shouted to them to let him go.
- Direct: He said, 'Be quite and listen to my words'.
- Indirect: He urged them to be quite and listen to his words.

Are you clear about the conversion of Direct to Indirect Speech?

H. How the Exclamation and the Wishes in the Direct Speeches are changed when the Direct Speeches are changed into Indirect Speeches?

In reporting exclamation and wishes, the Indirect Speech is introduced by some verb expressing Exclamation and Wishes.

Examples:

- Direct: He said, 'Alas! I am undone'.
- Indirect: He exclaimed sadly that he was undone.
- Direct: Alice said, 'How clever I am?'
- Indirect: Alice exclaimed that he was very clever.
- Direct: He said, 'Bravo! You have done well.'
- Indirect: He applauded him, saying that he had done well.
- Direct: 'So help me, Heaven!' he cried, 'I will never steal again'.
- Indirect: He called upon Heaven to witness his resolve never to resolve.

Chapter 16

Direct and Reported Speech

You can answer the question 'What did he/she say?' in two ways:

- by repeating the words spoken (direct speech)
- by reporting the words spoken (indirect or reported speech).

Direct Speech

Direct speech repeats, or quotes, the exact words spoken. When we use direct speech in writing, we place the words spoken between inverted commas ('....') and there is no change in these words. We may be reporting something that's being said NOW (for example a telephone conversation), or telling someone later about a previous conversation

Examples: She says, 'What time will you be home?'

She said, 'What time will you be home?'

and I said, 'I don't know! '

'There's a fly in my soup!' screamed Suresh.

Rahul said, 'There's an elephant outside the window.'

Reported Speech

Reported speech is usually used to talk about the past, so we normally change the tense of the words spoken. We use reporting verbs like 'say', 'tell', 'ask', and we may use the word 'that' to introduce the reported words. Inverted commas are not used.

She said, 'I saw him.' She said that she had seen him.

(a) 'That' may be omitted:

She told him that she was happy.

She told him she was happy.

(b) 'Say' and 'tell':

Use 'say' when there is no indirect object:

He said that he was tired.

Always use 'tell' when you say who was being spoken to (i.e. with an indirect object):

He told me that he was tired.

'Talk' and 'speak' are used:

- to describe the action of communicating:

He talked to us.

She was speaking on the telephone.

- with 'about' to refer to what was said:

He talked (to us) about his parents.

Hopes, Intentions, Promises in Reported Speech

When we report an intention, hope or promise, we use an appropriate reporting verb followed by a that-clause or a to-infinitive:

'I'll pay you the money tomorrow.'

He promised to pay me the money the next day.

He promised that he would pay me the money the next day.

Other verbs used in this pattern include:

hope, propose, threaten, guarantee, swear.

Examples:

(a) 'I'll be back by lunchtime.'

He promised to be back by lunchtime.

He promised that he would be back by lunchtime.

(b) 'We should arrive in London before nightfall.'

They hoped to arrive in London before nightfall.

They hoped they would arrive in London before nightfall.

(c) 'Give me the keys to the safe or I'll shoot you!'

He threatened to shoot me if I didn't give him the keys to the safe.

He threatened that he would shoot me if I didn't give him the keys to the safe.

Orders, Requests, Suggestions in Reported Speech

1. When we want to report an order or request, we can use a verb like 'tell' with a to-clause.

Examples:

He told me to go away.

The pattern is verb + indirect object + to-clause.

(The indirect object is the person spoken to.)

Other verbs used to report orders and requests in this way are: command, order, warn, ask, advise, invite, beg, teach, forbid.

Examples:

(a) The doctor said to me, 'Stop smoking!'.

The doctor told me to stop smoking.

(b) 'Get out of the car!' said the policeman.

The policeman ordered him to get out of the car.

(c) 'Could you please be quiet,' she said.

She asked me to be quiet.

(d) The man with the gun said to us, 'Don't move!'

The man with the gun warned us not to move.

2. Requests for objects are reported using the pattern ask + for + object: Examples:

(a) 'Can I have an apple?', she asked.

She asked for an apple.

(b) 'Can I have the newspaper, please?'

He asked for the newspaper.

(c) 'May I have a glass of water?' he said.

He asked for a glass of water.

(d) 'Sugar, please.'

She asked for the sugar.

(e) 'Could I have three kilos of onions?'

He asked for three kilos of onions.

3. Suggestions are usually reported with a that-clause. 'That' and 'should' are optional in these clauses:

She said: 'Why don't you get a mechanic to look at the car?'

She suggested that I should get a mechanic to look at the car. OR She suggested I get a mechanic to look at the car.

Other reporting verbs used in this way are: insist, recommend, demand, request, propose.

Examples:

(a) 'It would be a good idea to see the dentist', said my mother.

My mother suggested I see the dentist.

(*b*) The dentist said, 'I think you should use a different toothbrush'.

The dentist recommended that I should use a different toothbrush.

(*c*) My manager said, 'I think we should examine the budget carefully at this meeting.' My manager proposed that we examine the budget carefully at the meeting.

(*d*) 'Why don't you sleep overnight at my house?' she said.

She suggested that I sleep overnight at her house.

Notes: Suggest can also be followed by a gerund: I suggested postponing the visit to the dentist.

Questions in Reported Speech

1. Normal word order is used in reported questions, that is, the subject comes before the verb, and it is not necessary to use 'do' or 'did':

'Where does Paras live?'

She asked him where Paras lived.

2. Yes / no questions: This type of question is reported by using 'ask' + 'if / whether + clause:

(*a*) 'Do you speak English?'

He asked me if I spoke English.

(*b*) 'Are you British or Indian?'

He asked me whether I was British or Indian.

(*c*) 'Is it raining?'

She asked if it was raining.

(*d*) 'Have you got a computer?'

He wanted to know whether I had a computer.

(*e*) 'Can you type?'

She asked if I could type.

(f) 'Did you come by train?'

He enquired whether I had come by train.

(g) 'Have you been to Bristol before?'

She asked if I had been to Bristol before.

3. Question words: This type of question is reported by using 'ask' (or another verb like 'ask') + question word + clause. The clause contains the question, in normal word order and with the necessary tense change.

Examples:

(a) 'What is your name?' he asked me.

He asked me what my name was.

(b) 'How old is your mother?', he asked.

He asked how old her mother was.

(c) The mouse said to the elephant, 'Where do you live?'

The mouse asked the elephant where she lived.

(d) 'What time does the train arrive?' she asked.

She asked what time the train arrived.

(e) 'When can we have dinner?' she asked.

She asked when they could have dinner.

(f) The elephant said to the mouse, 'Why are you so small?'

The elephant asked the mouse why she was so small.

Part II Composition

Chapter 17

Essay Writing

Writing is an art you may not be able to grope instantly. It comes over a period of time and with constant practice. The word 'Essay' comes from the French word 'essai' that means effort and to sketch.

Types of Essay

There are many different types of essays and each warrants a different style of writing. Therefore the first thing to do is to focus on reason for writing the essay.

Narrative Essay

Narrative essays tell stories and hence, putting together a good narrative essay would require more simple wordings. For such essays, one must also employ their expressive powers well enough to be able to paint a clear picture for the readers so that they can actually see - rather than read about – a scene or a character in their own mind's eye.

Descriptive Essay

One of the most challenging forms of essay writing is writing descriptive essays. The best descriptive essays are those in which the writer knows and understands the subjects extremely well. The writer must then find the right words to project his or her views and imagery onto the readers of his or her work. The writer's choice of words has major importance because it would change the way, the reader visualizes or feels for the central object of the essay.

Persuasive Essay

Persuasive essay writing is all about being able to get the reader to see your viewpoint and to guide the reader to your way of thinking. Hence it is advisable to choose ideas for persuasive essay topics on the basis of what subjects move you the most. Since these essays require your motivation to be your driving force, you should make sure that you choose an essay that supports your own opinions on an issue.

Argumentative Essay

Argumentative essays present one side of an argument. The goal here is to be as convincing as possible so that the reader is influenced into adopting your line of thought. For writing argumentative essays effectively, one must first be sure of his or her own point-of-view on a subject. It can be really difficult to write an essay advocating a viewpoint that is not truly what you believe. Hence, it is advisable to pick a subject to write on that is not opposing to your own views and beliefs.

How to Write Essays?

Essay writing is an art of displaying information on a piece of paper that is intended to take a position in favour or against an issue. It can also be use as a tool to gather mass attention over a single point. Writing essays is a task that requires talent as well as technique of presentation and creating interest for readers to engage till the end. It doesn't mean that only select group of people with god gifted talent can write essay, but, it is a difficult job to do that's for sure. Here in this article, some tips that can help you in writing essays as well as avoiding common mistakes that beginners usually do.

1. **Plan you writing process:** Start with choosing an essay topic that you like most or are very strong over it. Now focus on your ideas, what you want reader to understand? Set an outline and stick to it till the end. Your outline ideally should include introduction, your view statement and conclusion, proofread and edit as per requirement.

2. **Stay on purpose:** Make sure that your essay meets all the requirements; it is focused on a single issue, easy to read and understand for general readers. Don't just provide information, rather give your arguments and try to illustrate your point in defined manner.

3. **Don't forget the basics:** It is important that you don't forget the basics of essay writing such as, managing your time by not involving in complex statements, answering the question clearly, and above all not providing copied material. Remember, people don't want to waste time on things which they can easily find on internet, you need to come up with original thoughts to maintain reader's interest.

Talking about essay writing tips, you need to avoid some common mistakes also, such as following:

1. **Don't put useless items:** Yes it sounds good to fill it up with loads of information to give away a decent impression of your knowledge and ability as a writer, but the reality is that people will just waste seconds to scroll down to decide whether they can digest all this useless items or not!

2. **Don't copy others ideas:** That's another famous policy

of beginners who seems to lack confidence on their own skills and search for cool ideas on internet and other sources. Today's readers are smart enough to pick the tone of essay, not just it will reduce your viewership, it will hurt your reputation very badly if you copy other peoples ideas without proper reference.

3. **Choosing an easy topic:** If it's easy for you to understand then it's same for other people also.. Always choose a topic that people wants to read about, but is not well supplied by writers.

Example Essays

Computer – Man's Greatest Invention

Man has made several inventions. Computer is one of them. The Computer has begun to control so many critical functions that man has prided on his inventions. Now, the computer plays an important role in our lives and we are completely dependent on him.

It has been commonly said that the computer can never replace the human brain, as it is created by humans but we cant ignore the fact that computer is much more capable than human brain. There are many ways in which the computer has the edge over man. The computer has the capability to evaluate problems that man can hardly imagine.

Even if a man can calculate the same problems as a computer, the computer can do it faster with 100% accuracy. The computer is clearly superior in many other aspects. In absolute speed of computation and retrieval of data, the computer is obviously by far the stronger. It has the capacity to handle things on a far bigger scale than the human brain could ever do.

Measurements, results, applications can all be done to the smallest details, far beyond the human brain's capabilities.

Calculations can be done with an accuracy nearly impossible. The human brain is easily stressed out by events and loses effectiveness when tired but computer can't.

On the other hand, the human brain has a lot of flaws, yet it also has an edge over the computer. It has the capacity to create, unlike the computer and it can work without full input, making logical assumptions about problems. A person can work with a wide variety of methods, seeing new, more efficient ways of handling problems.

It can come up with infinite ways of getting around problems encountered in day to day life, while a computer has a limited memory of new tricks it can come up with, limited by its programming. It is the human brain that figures out the programming that will allow any improvements for the computer. The human brain can learn to understand anything, it can grasp the central concept of anything.

Also, emotions are not capable in a computer. It allows the human brain to have evolved beyond a problem-solving machine. Emotions open the mind to an endless realm of possibilities. The reason why computers cannot create is because of the lack of emotions.

In conclusion, computers are far from perfect. They have only a limited capacity for learning .The computer lacks the common sense of the human brain. The human brain has many flaws just as it has advantages. The human brain can never perform tasks as efficiently or as tirelessly than the computer.

Emotions make the mind dangerously unstable, performance subject to moods and emotional disruption. The computer suffers no such problems.. Emotions blur the human brain's capacity to make clear, logical decisions. We can say that the computer is the best invention of man but only when it is operated with human brain .

Friendship

Friendship is a relationship that has many dimensions and styles. Friendship can be of between any two or persons and there is no compulsion of age, gender, geography, race, creed or nationality. People living in a house or living in this world are equally to prone to this relationship of friendship. Friendship has no boundaries and no limits.

In life every one will meet many people who say that they are your friend, but you will make only a few true friends. What is a friend? In the dictionary a friend is defined as one that is not hostile, or one attached to another by affection or esteem, a favoured companion. In my opinion a friend is much more than that. A friend is some one that will stand by you, even during the toughest times. Friendship is about believing in your friends and helping them to achieve all they can or want to do in life. We are there for each other with hugs, advice, kind words, fights, and anger, whatever comes along. When the day ends, we are still friends who have each other no matter what happens.

We all have a desire to have friends. It is what makes us reach out of our shells and take the chance of being hurt. It is not easy figuring out who is a friend and who is not. I believe Divya, to be a true friend. We meet in high school and have known each other for five years. Divya and I have been through many good and hard times together. In addition, we have experienced so many adventures together, such as traveling to Italy and the Caribbean where we shared so many enjoyable adventures. Are friendship has done nothing but grow and continues to do so. We are currently indulgencing in another adventure by living together in Ottawa, and are going to be attending Carleton University in September.

I consider Divya to be a true friend. A true friend is there for you when you need them. To have a true friend is a remarkable thing. To find someone that shares similar interests, who cares about whom you are and what you are doing. A true friend is there for you when you need them.

Someone who you are not embarrassed to cry in front of, who you can tell the deepest darkest secrets to and know they will be safe. An old rule of thumb is that a true friend is someone you can call after months or ever years and speak as if not a day had passed.

Divya and I have experienced this, we were parted from each other for about a year and half while she was away at her first year university and I moved back to my home India to spend some time with my mom. Once we came in contact again with each other to attend university it was as though we never skipped a beat.

True friendships come along so rarely, and I am so thankful to have met her that we must move past anything that threatens them and see the big picture. Without our friendships, we are indeed lost.

Whatever happens, we should always keep our true friends close to our heart. Tell them how much they mean to you. Do not let them slip away. If they do, go out and get them back. The bonds we make during these days will serve to keep us going in the months and years ahead.

Elections – Foundation of Democracy

Elections form the foundation of democracy. They are the central institution of democratic representative governments. It is not only legal but also a moral responsibility of a democratic nation to hold free and fair elections. It is true that all modern democracies hold elections.

But on the same time it is also true that all elections are not democratic. Right-wing dictatorships, communalist, and single-party governments also stage elections to make their rule. Such parties represent only one candidate or a list of candidates. Such circumstances allow no alternative choices to the voter.

Though such elections may offer several candidates for each office, it is usually ensured through pressure or supports that only the government approved candidate is chosen. Other elections may offer genuine choices – but only within the serving party. These are not democratic elections.

Democratic Elections

'Democratic elections are competitive, periodic, comprehensive, definitive elections in which the chief decision-makers in a government are selected by citizens who enjoy broad freedom to criticise government, to publish their criticism and to present alternatives' says Jeane Kirkpatrick, scholar and former U.S. ambassador to the United Nations.

Democratic elections are **competitive**. The opposition, whether it consists of one party or many as well as all the candidates in an election must enjoy the freedom of speech, assembly, and movement necessary to speak their mind. A true democracy allows criticisms of the government. Democracy also allows all the parties to bring alternative policies and candidates to the voters. Simply permitting all access to the ballot is not enough in a true democracy. A democracy in which all the parties are not allowed a fair use of media to generate awareness in the public regarding their view, agenda etc. certainly cannot be called a democracy.

Moreover a country where the campaigning rallies of the candidates or the parties other than the ruling one are harassed or where newspapers indulge in yellow journalism victimizing a particular candidate or a party also cannot be called democratic. The party in power may enjoy the advantages of incumbency, but the rules and conduct of the election contest must be fair.

Democratic elections are **periodic**. A democracy like India holds elections after a specific period of time. In India, polling time is after every five years. Democracies do not elect dictators or presidents-for-life. Even a successfully running government is required to seek the approval of the common man after its term is over. Moreover, the elected officials are answerable to the people as it is the same people whose votes hold the power to elect them again or choose a new government. Thus it is quite obvious that the elected government cannot go on fooling the people with empty promises. The promises made to the common man are to be fulfilled else the power would slip out of the hands of the government resulting into a new government.

Democratic elections are **comprehensive**. The definition of citizen and voter must be large enough to include a large proportion of the adult population. A government chosen by a small, exclusive group is not a democracy. Thus all the members of the minorities irrespective of racial tribal, or religious factors or women should be allowed full citizenship with the right to vote.

Democratic elections are **definitive**. They determine the leadership of the government. The elected representatives rule subject to the laws and constitution of the country. Democracies flourish in the act of voting itself. To cast a pressure free ballot, voters in a democracy must be permitted to cast their ballots in secret. Thus the votes are confidential. At the same time, the protection of the ballot box and tallying of vote totals must be conducted as openly as possible, so that citizens are confident that the results are accurate.

Global Warming

Global warming is an increase in the average temperature of the earth's temperature, especially a sustained change sufficient to cause climate change. The average facade temperature of the globe has increased more than 1 degree since 1900 and the speed of warming has been almost three folds the century long average since 1970. This increase in earth's average temperature is called Global Warming. More or less all specialists studying the climate record of the earth have the same opinion now that human actions, mainly the discharge of green house gases from smokestacks, vehicles, and burning forests, are perhaps the leading power driving the fashion. The gases append to the planet's normal greenhouse effect, permitting sunlight in, but stopping some of the ensuing heat from burning back to space.

Based on the study on past climate shifts, notes of current situations, and computer simulations, many climate scientists say that lacking of big curbs in greenhouse gas discharges, the 21st century might see temperatures rise of about 3 to 8 degrees, climate patterns piercingly shift, ice sheets contract and seas rise several feet. With the probable exemption of one more world war, a huge asteroid, or a fatal plague, global warming may be the only most danger to our planet earth.

Global Warming Causes

The major cause of global warming is the release of green house gases like carbon dioxide, methane, nitrous oxide etc into the atmosphere. The major source of carbon dioxide is the power plants. These power plants emit large amounts of carbon dioxide produced from burning of fossil fuels for the purpose of electricity generation. About twenty percent of carbon dioxide emitted in the atmosphere comes from burning of gasoline in the engines of the vehicles. Buildings, both commercial and residential represent a larger source of global warming pollution than cars and trucks.

Building of these structures require a lot of fuel to be burnt which emits a large amount of carbon dioxide in the atmosphere. Methane is more than 20 times as effectual as CO^2 at entrapping heat in the atmosphere. Methane is obtained from resources such as rice paddies, bovine flatulence, bacteria in bogs and fossil fuel manufacture.

The main sources of nitrous oxide include nylon and nitric acid production, cars with catalytic converters, the use of fertilisers in agriculture and the burning of organic matter. Another cause of global warming is deforestation that is caused by cutting and burning of forests for the purpose of residence and industrialisation.

Scientists all over the world are making predictions about the ill effects of Global Warming and connecting some of the events that have taken place in the past few decades as an alarm of Global Warming. The effect of Global Warming is increasing the average temperature of the earth. A rise in earth's temperatures can in turn root to other alterations in the ecology, including an increasing sea level and modifying the quantity and pattern of rainfall.

These modifications may boost the occurrence and concentration of severe climate events, such as floods, famines, heat waves, tornados, and twisters. Other consequences may comprise of higher or lower agricultural outputs, glacier melting, lesser summer stream flows, genus extinctions and rise in the ranges of disease vectors. As an effect of Global Warming some species like has already become extinct.

As an effect of Global Warming various new diseases have emerged latterly. It is expected that many species will die off or become extinct due to the increase in the temperatures of the water, whereas various other species, which prefer warmer waters, will increase tremendously. Perhaps the most disturbing changes are expected in the coral reefs that are expected to die off as an effect of Global Warming. The Global Warming is expected to cause irreversible changes in the ecosystem and the behaviour of animals. Birds are a species that will be affected by a change in the climate. Global Warming might result in birds finding a more permanent home in northern areas in the Northern Hemisphere.

The scientists tell us that the tundra is in danger of melting holds an amount of extra global warming pollution that is equivalent to the net amount that is previously in the earth's atmosphere. Likewise, earlier one more team of scientists reported that the in a single year Greenland witnessed 32 glacial earthquakes between 4.6 and 5.1 on the Richter scale.

This is a disturbing sign and points that a huge destabilisation that may now be in progress deep within the second biggest growth of ice on the planet. This ice would be enough to raise sea level 20 feet worldwide if it broke up and slipped into the sea. Each day passing brings yet new proof that we are now in front of a global emergency, a climate emergency that needs instant action to shrilly decrease carbon dioxide emissions worldwide in order to turn down the earth's rising temperatures and avoid any calamity.

It is not easy to attach any particular events to Global Warming, but studies prove the fact that human activities are increasing the earth's temperature. Even though most predictions focus on the epoch up to 2100, even if no further greenhouse gases were discharged after this date, Global Warming and sea level would be likely to go on to rise for more than a millennium, since carbon dioxide has a long average atmospheric life span.

Many efforts are being made by various nations to cut

down the rate of Global Warming. One such effort is the Kyoto agreement that has been made between various nations to reduce the emissions of various green house gases. Also many non-profit organisations are working for the cause. Al Gore was one of the foremost U.S. politicians to heave an alarm about the hazards of Global Warming. He has produced a significantly acclaimed documentary movie called 'An Inconvenient Truth,' and written a book that archives his advice that Earth is dashing toward an immensely warmer future. Al Gore, the former vice president of United States has given various speeches to raise an awareness of Global Warming. He has warned people about the ill effects of Global Warming and its remedies.

The future of emissions damage depends on several factors, demographics, economics, technology, policies and institutional developments. Future predictions do not look good for this planet if nothing is done.

Father of Nation

Mohandas Karamchand Gandhi, commonly known as the Father of Nation, was a great Freedom Fighter. He was born in the town of Porbander in Gujarat on 2 October 1869. He had done his schooling in nearby Rajkot. At that time India was under Britishs. His father died before Gandhi could finish his schooling, and at thirteen he was married to Kasturba who was even younger. In 1888, Gandhi set sail for England, where he had decided to pursue a degree in law.

After one year of a none too successful law practice, Gandhi decided to accept an offer from an Indian businessman in South Africa, Dada Abdulla, to join him as a legal adviser. The Indians who had been living in South Africa were without political rights, and were generally known by the derogatory name of 'coolies'.

Gandhi himself came to an awareness of the frightening force when he thrown out of a first-class railway compartment car, though he held a first-class ticket, at Pietermaritzburg. From this political awakening Gandhi was to emerge as the leader of the Indian community, and it is in South Africa that he first coined the term *satyagraha* to signify his theory and practice of non-violent resistance.

Gandhi was to describe himself as a seeker of *satya* (truth), which could not be attained other than through *ahinsa* (non-violence, love) and *brahmacharya* (celibacy, striving towards God).

Gandhi returned to India in early 1915, and was never to leave the country. Over the next few years, he was to become involved in numerous local struggles, such as at Champaran in Bihar, where workers on indigo plantations complained of oppressive working conditions, and at Ahmedabad, where a dispute had broken out between management and workers at textile mills.

Gandhi had ideas on every subject, from hygiene and nutrition to education and labour, and he relentlessly pursued his ideas in newspaper. He would still be remembered as one of the principal figures in the history of Indian journalism.

By this time he had earned the title of *Mahatma* from Rabindranath Tagore, India's most well-known writer. When tragedy happened in the Jallianwala Bagh in Amritsar Gandhi wrote the report of the Punjab Congress Inquiry Committee.

Over the next two years, Gandhi initiated the non-cooperation movement, which called upon Indians to withdraw from British institutions, to return honours conferred by the British, and to learn the art of self-reliance; though the British administration was at places paralyzed, the movement was suspended in February 1922.

In early 1930, the Indian National Congress, declared that it would now be satisfied with nothing short of complete independence (*purna swaraj*).

On March 2, Gandhi addressed a letter to the Viceroy, Lord Irwin, informing him that unless Indian demands were met, he would be compelled to break the 'salt laws'. On the early morning of March 12, with a small group of followers towards Dandi on the sea.

They arrived there on April 5th: Gandhi picked up a small lump of natural salt, and so gave the signal to hundreds of thousands of people to similarly defy the law, since the British exercised a monopoly on the production and sale of salt. This was the beginning of the civil disobedience movement.

In 1942, Gandhi issued the last call for independence from British rule. On the grounds of *Kranti Maidan*, he delivered a speech, asking every Indian to lay down their life, if necessary, in the cause of freedom. He gave them this mantra: 'Do or

Die'; at the same time, he asked the British to 'Quit India'. After a long struggle India got his independence on 15th August 1947.

One evening Gandhiji was late to his prayers. At 10 minutes past 5 o'clock, with one hand each on the shoulders of Abha and Manu, who were known as his 'walking sticks', Gandhi commenced his walk towards the garden.

Gandhi folded his hands and greeted his audience with a namaskar; at that moment, a young man came up to him took a revolver out of his pocket, and shot Gandhi three times in his chest. Bloodstains appeared over Gandhi's white woollen shawl; his hands still folded in a greeting, Gandhi blessed his assassin: *He Ram! He Ram! And left us.*

Drugs – The Killer of Youth

The start of college is a new and different experience for all teenagers. They are keen to learn about their new surroundings and make new friends. Many teens attract to drink, smoke and drugs to be considered as cool.

In a survey recently conducted on the abuse of alcohol, nicotine, and other harmful drugs, we studied that the maximum number of teenagers involved in smoking, drinking and drugs are in the age group from fourteen to twenty.

In today's society, the pressure to drink, smoke or use drugs to fit in is all around our youth.

On the basis of survey, it was found that these teenagers drink one to two times per week because they enjoy it. They feel that it is also a chance to have fun and hang out with their friends. However, teens say they also do it out of boredom. Often, teens are anxious to find an alternative way to have fun and to escape from the 'boringness' of movies and television. For this reason they jump at the chance together in a large group to socialise. They are willing to pay their pocket money for a cup of beer, even if they known that drinking under age is illegal.

Drinking alcohol comes with many responsibilities. These teens define 'responsible drinking' as 'having control of your actions'. In other words, teens drink as long as they know what they are doing. While drinking teenagers are often put into situations where they act irresponsible.

Teenagers are often caught driving while under the influence of alcohol. When teens get into the car, they often do not think about the consequences. There is always that one thought in the back of everyone's mind in this type of situation. They say, 'Nothing' bad is going to happen. Sadly, when something does happen, most of the time the drunk driver is never the one to be injured. It is always the innocent passengers or the victims on the road.

Smoking is another large issue within the college community. Many teenagers who smoke have been smoking for a few years and started smoking at an early age. Even though most people do not agree with teens smoking, a good percentage of adults smoke cigarettes. Therefore, the influence to smoke is constantly around teens and young children. On the other hand, some teens also like to smoke socially. This usually occurs at parties or just when they feel like hanging around outside of their dorms.

Drug usage is the third huge area of abuse among students in college. The majority of these teens have tried the most common gateway drug, marijuana. Many of these teenagers said they have also tried mushrooms, ecstasy, and speed.

Peer pressure has nothing to do with their reasons for drinking, smoking, or doing drugs. They believe college is the time to live. Drinking alcohol, smoking cigarettes, and using drugs are not going to stop them from having the times of their lives. Only awareness can stop them.

Science *v/s* Religion

Science and religion, we always here contradictory on these two. It is very difficult to choose one over the other because one is based on fact and logic while the other is built on faith and hope. That's exactly what the Creation theory is, beliefs in a superior supernatural being whereas the Big Bang theory is faith in logic. It is difficult to judge two uniquely difficult theories because both do not hold the answers, they are merely a description of the type of person we are, and what morals and priorities we have with us. Someone who is atheist for example will believe in the scientific version; whereas someone who has had a bad life may hold onto their hope for a being that will one day make the world better for them, and hence they will trust the theory of religion. But it's not easy to choose between the two.

Normally when approached with a task of choice, we will subject ourselves to view every different side to each story to make an intelligible decision based on the truth. Unfortunately, with this topic we cannot. As a student, it is solely based on our personal beliefs, but where have these beliefs evolved in the first place? As we grew with each stage in our lives, we had been influenced by an outside force.

Whether it be our parents, the media, our school systems– our ideas are truly not our own. How can one make an unbiased opinion with all these factors to consider? It is impossible. I grew up as a Catholic, I went to a Catholic Church all my life, my mom whom I believe is as close to a fundamentalist as they come, taught me the Creation story, my teachers at my Catholic schools taught me the same theory and so on. Of course, I am going to believe the Creation theory, I was brainwashed to believe it, and even if it is the wrong choice, I will always believe it. Even as an older pupil with an independence and a mind of my own, I still believe this, it is my faith, I learned that it was right and hence, until my death, no one will change my opinion (unless with the answers of course!) because once it's in my mind, it will never leave.

However, there is always the logical aspect to this. As you develop your mind, you start asking yourself philosophical questions, questions that have no answer and possible answers seem to contradict one another. This is where my other sense of perception can alter my already existing theory. I think that although science has not actually began creation, they continued it. I am skeptical about the Adam and Eve theory, not that I doubt God's abilities, but there are gaps in that theory too.

Therefore, I think God created the universe, the plant life and the animals. He created everything. But I think humans were not derived from dust like the Bible states. I believe God created the animals which evolved into humans. If not that, than I believe he created apes to be the first humans but saw they were not as advanced as they could be. So He altered them slightly and then humans were made. Possibly Adam and Eve were the first humans to exist, the Bible states God created them last anyway. Or possibly I'm wrong. Whatever the case may be, the answer is out there, but no one will ever find it.

Nuclear Power

Nuclear Power is a source of energy which has many benefits. Nuclear energy is less expensive because it is based on uranium. With little amount of uranium a great amount of energy can be produced. It is a reliable source to rely on as there is significant amount of it on the Earth's crust.

One important advantage is that producing energy using Nuclear Power does not give off Greenhouse gases. Green house gases are gases like carbon dioxide and sulphur dioxide which are contributing to the Greenhouse effect or Global Warming. The biggest advantage of Nuclear Power is the discoveries made in Nuclear Medicine, such as cancer therapy, CAT scan and MRI machines and the use of irradiation of food to kill bacteria.

Nuclear Power has been used in the last hundred years for the manufacture of Nuclear Weapons like A-Bombs (atomic bombs) and H-Bombs (hydrogen bombs). Nuclear Weapons are weapons of mass destruction. A single weapon can be capable of destroying an entire city. In the history of warfare Nuclear Weapons have been used on two occasions, both during the closing days of World War II in Hiroshima when a devise called 'Little Boy' was dropped and then three days later one in Nagasaki called 'Fat Man'. It is a good idea to possess Nuclear Weapons if you are a 'Super Power'. If a country feels threatened it can rely on Nuclear Weapons to protect them from the enemy. Examples of 'Nuclear Super Powers' are USA, Russia, United Kingdom, China, France etc.

Nuclear Weapons have many disadvantages. The use of them can lead to a world crisis as every time a bomb explodes the lives of millions of people are affected. Nuclear Weapons are very expensive to manufacture even though the uranium is accessible.

India-US Nuclear Deal

India -USA Nuclear Deal brought about lots of hopes and aspirations to the vast multitudes of energy starved people of

India. It forged a new dynamic, vibrant, business relationship with the only super power of the planet —The USA..

After the initial euphoria created by the July 18 deal, few of our intellectuals started dreaming (rightly) that India is on the verge of becoming a superpower .They fell aghast when new conditions started creeping in . The MAY 2nd agreement attempted to fix the goalposts and remove any kind of vague discrepancies. With vigilant media staring straight in the eyes , stiff opposition from political parties and dynamic watchdog - nuclear scientific community putting forth periodic clarifications and suggestions , the whole of India was participating in this GREAT PUBLIC DEBATE ....should we have it or leave it.

India is one of the counties that is part of the global endeavour to master nuclear fusion technologies. Along with USA, Japan, S. Korea , France , Germany and China , its part of a pioneering research in TOKMAK technologies. Nuclear fusion energy is cheap, and environmental friendly. We are competent enough to achieve significant breakthroughs in any kind of technology if only given the Time and Money !

One major disadvantage of Nuclear Power is that it makes variable amounts of radioactive waste. This waste is causing big problems for the world storage because of its irradiation. The nuclear waste has to be stored over a hundred years and the waste remains hot for thousands of years. Some people say Nuclear energy is cheaper to make but this is not the entire truth. Although Nuclear Power has many disadvantages I think it is necessary as long as it is used for a good cause. The fossil fuels we are currently using for making energy are some day going to run out so we need other sources. If Nuclear Power is handled correctly the possibility of an accident is very rare.

I think Nuclear Power is a good substitute to burning fossil fuels for energy as it does not contribute to Global Warming. Nuclear Weapons not only cause massive destruction, the money that countries invest for the manufacturing and testing of these weapons can be used to feed millions of poor people.

Good Leader

A good leader is the one who can get the things done by his team, with the optimum support from them. A leader should gain the support of the team, not in force. But it should come from the heart of the team. The leader should have such motivation skills to get the support from the team. Enforcing the power to get the things done cannot work for long duration. That would make the team to work without interest, that too for small duration. We saw many autocrat leaders in the history who ruled the people as per their wish. But they could not be the successful leaders.

The democrat leader is one, who takes the opinion of the people before taking any decision. That would really encourage the team members to support the leader. That would bring the feeling of involvement to the team members. But if a leader is taking his own decision without consulting the team members, and if he is just enforcing that to the team, that would really bring the disobedience kind of reactions in the team.

In the history we have seen many democrat leaders like Mahatma Gandhi, Nelson Mandela, Abraham Lincoln etc. people who have gained the support of the people and achieved the miracles. We should make them as the examples to follow. There is a traditional definition of management that 'The management is what a manager does'. But that concept is nowhere relevant. Even if applied, won't stay for long time. So the management should be taken as an art of getting the whole hearted support from the team to get the things done by them.

What makes a good leader?

The leadership qualities that are required to make a good leader can vary in different companies, teams and situations.

This can be illustrated in both art and modern leadership models. For example, the fact that leadership qualities are dependent on context is demonstrated in the play The Admirable Crichton and the film Twelve O' Clock High.

In 'The Admirable Crichton', written in 1902, the Lord and butler swap their roles as leader and servant as the situation changes. On a desert island, the butler's practical skills are essential for survival, whereas the Lord's knowledge of English politics is of no value.

In the film 'Twelve O' Clock High', produced in 1949, as a squadron starts to suffer increasing losses during the war, the leader's people-oriented approach starts to fail. He is replaced by a dictatorial bully who turns the squadron round and restores their pride.

Leadership Styles

Some people have one style of leadership, which is fine if they can find a situation that requires that style of leadership.

Flexible leadership, however, involves being able to adapt your leadership style according to the situation and the state of the team - e.g. taking charge when a team is forming but playing the role of coach when a team is managing itself well.

Perspective

How you approach leadership qualities will depend on whether you are looking at the subject from the perspective of an organisation or an individual.

Organisations aim to improve their performance by selecting and developing individual potential. At the outset, the needs of the organisation are usually well-defined but the individuals, who may become leaders, are unknown. The organisational task is therefore one of:

- identifying the profile of people who will enhance organisational performance
- selecting individuals whose character, skills and potential closely match that profile

- developing those individuals so their potential becomes a reality:

  That is, an organisation develops a framework to assess people and develop those who are chosen.

  An individual's perspective, however, is very different: the aim is for the individual to develop into a position of leadership. You are who you are, and if your profile does not fit that of the organisation you are working for, then your task is to:

- understand your own attributes or potential.
- find a new role or organisation where your profile will be valued

Conclusion

What makes a good leader? The answer depends on the context. Organisations need to find people who have what they are looking for. Individuals need to find organisations who are looking for what they have to offer. See the basics of leadership for discussion of the different between leadership and management

Dowry System

Dowry is derived from the ancient Hindu customs of 'kanyadan' and 'stridhan'. In 'kanyadan', the father of the bride offers the father of the groom money or property, etc. whereas for 'stridhan', the bride herself gets jewelry and clothes at the time of her marriage, usually from her relatives or friends. In 'varadakshina', the father of the bride presents the groom cash or kind. All of these could be done voluntarily and out of affection and love.

The Hindu marriage system is sacramental. According to this system, a marriage is forever, and there is no scope for a separation. Among the various ceremonies previously practiced, the ceremony in front of a 'godly' fire ('Yajna' in Sanskrit) has taken over, the old-fashioned system of 'marrying a wife by capture.

This form of marriage began the practice of dowry, where originally, the family of the bride would accept gifts and money from the groom's family as an alternative to bloodshed during the capture of the bride. A later modification of this system has paved way for the present dowry system primarily practiced by the society.

The dowry custom continues to rule society. In majority of Indian families the boy has legacy rights while the girl is given a large sum at the time of her marriage in lieu of the Government regulated equal rights for girls in parental property. Thus dowry system has spread in almost all parts of the country and sections of society.

There are several reasons for the occurrence of the dowry system, but the main one is that it is a necessary precondition for marriage. 'No dowry, no marriage,' is a widespread fear. There has also been an appearance of a feudal mindset with a materialistic attitude in a new globalised economy. The price tag for the groom is now bigger and bolder. The emergence of an affluent middle class, the torchbearer of social change in modern India, is the main factor for the continuation of the dowry system.

Families arrange most marriages, and a man who does not marry for love he can marry for wealth. For this man, and his family, a woman becomes the ticket to shortcut riches through the system of dowry.

There are a number of things people desire to have in their own houses but cannot afford; they use the opportunity of a son's marriage to get them. The girl's parents do not protest against variety, as they regard the union as a stepping-stone towards higher social status and better matches for the remaining children.

Dowry as a phenomenon has gone beyond the ritual of marriage. Pregnancy, childbirth and all kinds of religious and family functions are occasions when such demands are made. A more sophisticated public image of an extended gifting session has replaced the old system.

Now there is demand for receptions in marriage palaces. The trousseau includes designer wear for the bride and groom's family. Chefs are flown in for multi-cuisine wedding dinners. The bride's family usually pays for all this. The rich revel in the exchange of their black money, but this in turn exerts pressure on the other classes to ape them with serious social consequences.

The women have become a kind of commodity. It is them who are the worst sufferers because dowry is most often a monetary agreement between two men – the bride's father and the groom. Caste-based practices have only added fuel to the fire. Marriages in political families are arranged to consolidate the caste base for support in electoral politics, so they do not challenge the dowry system.

Dowry rituals have now spread even to communities where

they were unknown. It has gone to different castes, crossed the boundaries of provinces and education and religion. Muslims and Christians, such as the Syrian Christians of Kerala and the Roman Catholics of Mangalore have started demanding dowry.

Official statistics show a steady rise in dowry crimes. Thousands of women are killed every year in India over dowry. Bihar and Uttar Pradesh still record the maximum number of dowry crimes, but Bangalore, India's fastest growing city also shows an alarming rise – four women reportedly die every day because of dowry harassment and domestic violence. The cases of dowry torture are the highest accounting for 32.4% of crimes against women in the country.

The Dowry Prohibition Act, in force since 1st July 1961, was passed with the purpose of prohibiting the demanding, giving and taking of dowry. In 1980 the Government set-up a committee which recommended amendments in the Dowry Prohibition Act and also suggested expanding the definition of dowry and instituting family courts and National Commission for Women.

Many parliamentary debates led to some amendments in 1983,1984 and 1986. To stop the offences of cruelty by husband or his relatives on the wife, Section 498-A was added in the Indian Penal Code and Section 198-A in the Criminal Procedure Code in the year 1983.

The Dowry Prohibition Act clearly stipulates that a person who gives or takes or helps in the giving or taking of dowry can be sentenced to jail for 5 years and fined Rs.15,000/- or the amount of the value of dowry, whichever is more.

The Act also prohibits the giving and taking directly or indirectly any property or valuable security, any amount either in cash of kind, jewelry, articles, properties, etc. in respect of a marriage. The control is provided by stating a limit and names of gifters and their relationship to the married couple to be signed by both sides of parents.

In 1986, the Act was amended again, empowering State governments to appoint Dowry Prohibition Officers, who not only had a preventive role but also had powers to collect evidence against people who took dowry.

Despite protest by women's organisations, serious activism, legal amendments, special police cells for women, media support and heightened awareness of dowry being a crime, the practice continues unabated on a massive scale.

Despite every stigma, dowry continues to be the signature of marriage. Women need real social, political, financial and moral support in their fight against the system. They have to be empowered so that they can take their decisions about their own life by refusing the dowry system.

Indian Women

In Indian society, the status of women has changed from time to time; position of women in society is the index to the standard of social organisation. We can divide the past into three phases to analyse the status of women. They are Ancient India , Medieval India and Modern Indian period.

Ancient Indian Women

In ancient India women enjoyed equal status with man in all fields of life, she received the same education like man, many Hindu religious books like Vedas, Upanishads, Ramayana, Mahabharata have mentioned the names of several women who were great scholars, poets, philosophers of the time. The wife was 'Ardhangini' which means she is half of her husband. An unmarried man was considered to be incomplete man. All religious ceremonies were performed by the husband along with the wife. This shows the importance given to the women in ancient period.

Medieval Period Indian Women

But in the Medieval period, the status of women went down considerably. She was considered to be inferior to man. Any historians have called this age as the 'dark age'. Her position became very miserable. Decline in the status of women in Indian society begins with the Muslims rule in India: customs of pardha, sati, child marriage and restrictions on widow marriage are prevalence of joint family system have been the factors responsible for the injustice done towards women. These problems related with women resulted in changed mindset of people. Now they began to consider a girl as misery and a burden, which has to be secured from the eyes of intruders and needs extra care. All this gave rise to some new evils such as Child Marriage, Sati, Jauhar and restriction on girl education

Sati: The ritual of dying at the funeral pyre of the husband is known as 'Sati' or 'Sahagaman'. According to some of the Hindu scriptures women dying at the funeral pyre of her husband go straight to heaven so its good to practice this ritual. Sati was considered to be the better option then living as a widow as the plight of widows in Hindu society was even worse.

Jauhar: It is also more or less similar to Sati but it is a mass suicide. Jauhar was prevalent in the Rajput societies. In this custom wives immolated themselves while their husband were still alive. When people of Rajput clan became sure that they were going to die at the hands of their enemy then all the women arrange a large pyre and set themselves afire.

Child Marriage: It was a norm in medieval India. Girls were married off at the age of 8-10. They were not allowed access to education and were treated as the material being. The child marriage along with it brought some more problems such as increased birth rate, poor health of women due to repeated child bearing and high mortality rate of women and children.

Restriction on Widow Remarriage: The condition of widows in medieval India was very bad. They were not treated as human beings and were subjected to a lot of restrictions. They were supposed to live pious life after their husband died and were not allowed entry in any celebration.

Purdah System: The veil or the 'Purdah' system was widely prevalent in medieval Indian society. It was used to protect the women folk from the eyes of foreign rulers who invaded India in medieval period. But this system curtailed the freedom of women.

Girl Education: The girls of medieval India and especially Hindu society were not given formal education. They were given education related to household chores.

Though these evils were present in medieval Indian society but they were mainly confined to Hindu society. As compared to Hindu society other societies such as Buddhism, Jainism and Christians were a bit lenient. Women in those societies enjoyed far more freedom. The status of women in Southern India was better than the North India. While in Northern India there were not many women administrators, in Southern India we can find some names that made women of that time proud. There was one major evil present in South India of medieval time. It was the custom of Devadasis.

Devadasis: It was a custom prevalent in Southern India. In this system girls were dedicated to temples in the name of gods and goddesses. All the requirements of Devadasis were fulfilled by the grants given to the temples. In temple they used to spend their time in worship of god and by singing and dancing for the god. Some kings used to invite temple dancers to perform at their court for the pleasure of courtiers and thus some Devadasis converted to Rajadasis (palace dancers) prevalent in some tribes of South India like Yellamma cult.

Women's Struggle and Reforms

Though women of India are not at par with her counterpart in Western world but she is struggling hard to make her mark in men's world. We can count on certain names from the British India where women put the example of extraordinary bravery which even men might not be able to show. Rani Lakshmi Bai of Jhansi was the one such woman. There have many social reformers who have helped women gain their previous status in society.

Raja Ram Mohan Roy: He was strictly against the evils prevalent in society in his time. He is the one who has done women a great favour by abolishing Sati lawfully. Ram Mohan Roy also did great work in the field of women education. He was against child marriage and favoured widow remarriage.

Ishwar Chandra Vidyasagar: Ishwar Chandra Vidyasagar was popularly known as Vidyasagar, which means sea of knowledge. He strongly supported women education in Bengal and went door to door to persuade people to send their girl child to school. He also did a lot in the field of widow remarriage. He opened many schools for girls.

Mahatma Jyotirao Phule: He was the one to open first girl school in India. He is also credited with opening first home for widows of the upper caste and a home for newborn girl children so that they can be saved from female infanticide.

Swami Dayananda Saraswati: He emphasised for the equal rights for women in every field. He tried to change the mindset of people with his Vedic teachings.

Mahatma Gandhi: He was the one who liberated Indian women from the clutches of 'Purdah' and other social evils.

Modern Indian Women

The status of women in modern India is a sort of a irony. If on one hand she is at the peak of ladder of success, on the other hand she is suffering the violence afflicted on her by her own family members. As compared with past women in modern times have achieved a lot but in reality they have to still travel a long way. Their path is full of roadblocks. The women have left the secured domain of their home and are now in the battlefield of life, fully armored with their talent. There are many problems which women in India have to go through daily. These problems have become the part and parcel of life of Indian women and some of them have accepted them as their fate.

The main problems of Indian women includes:

Malnutrition: Generally in India, women are the one who eat last and least in the whole family. So they eat whatever is left after men folk are satiated. As a result most of the times their food intake does not contain the nutritional value required in maintaining the healthy body. In villages, sometimes women do not get to eat the whole meal due to poverty.

Poor Health: The malnutrition results in poor health of women. The women of India are prejudiced from the birth itself. They are not breastfed for long. In the want of a son the women wants to get pregnant as soon as possible which decreases the caring period to the girl child whereas the male members get adequate care and nutrition.

Maternal Mortality: The mortality rate in India is among highest in the world. As females are not given proper attention, which results in the malnutrition and then they are married at an early age which leads to pregnancies at younger age when the body is not ready to bear the burden of a child. All this results in complications, which may lead to gynaecological problems, which may become serious with time and may ultimately, lead to death.

Lack of education: In India women education never got its due share of attention. The people of villages consider girls to be curse and they do not want to waste money and time on them as they think that women should be wedded off as soon as possible.

Mistreatment - In India violence against women is a common evil. Not just in remote parts but in cities also women bear the brunt. They are subjected to physical and mental violence.

Overworked: Indian women work more than men of India but their work is hardly recognized as they mainly do unskilled work. Their household chores is never counted as a work, if a woman is working in a field to help her husband it will also be not counted as a work.

Lack of power: In India a large percentage of women do not have power. They cannot take decisions independently not even related to their own life. They have to take permission of male members for each and every issue. They don't have any say in important household matters and not in matter of their own marriage.

Marriage: The family mainly fixes the marriages in India. The scenario in villages is very bad. Going against the wishes of husband is considered to be a sin. In marriage husband always has the upper hand.

Dowry: Courts are flooded with cases related to death due to dowry harassment by husband and in laws. Due to this evil practice many newlywed women of India have to lose their lives.

Female infanticide/foeticide: As women were supposed to be and in some areas of India are still considered to be curse by some strata of society their birth was taken as a burden.

Divorce: It is regarded as the sign of failure of marriage, especially of women. She is treated as if she has committed some crime by divorcing her husband.

Current Scenario: The position of women in modern India has changed considerably. Her position in modern Indian society is equal to that of men, socially, economically, educationally, politically and legally. Now, she has the right to receive education, inherit and own property, participate in public life and political life of the nation. She has become economically independent. She can seek employment anywhere and remains not a domestic slave. So, she is certainly enjoying the equal status with man in all respect.

Some Bright Spots: India has world's largest number of professionally qualified women.

India has largest population of working women in the world.

India has more number of doctors, surgeons, scientists, professors than the United States.

Women Achiever: Today, Indian women have excelled in each and every field from social work to visiting space station. There is no arena, which remained unconquered by Indian women. Whether it is politics, sports, entertainment, literature, technology everywhere we can hear applauses for her.

Politics: Women of India are highly active today in this area. Sarojini Naidu, Vijaylakshami Pandit, Sucheta Kriplani were the torchbearer for the women of India. Vijayalkshami Pandit was the first Indian woman to hold a post in the cabinet. The most important name in the category of women politicians of recent times is Mrs Indira Gandhi. Today her daughter-in law Mrs Sonia Gandhi is following her footsteps and leading the Indian National Congress. Other women who have made their name in politics of India are Shiela Dixit, Uma Bharti, Jayalalitha, Vasundhra Raje, Mayavati and Mamata Banerjee.

Sports

Indian women have achieved great laurels for the nation in every sport. Whether it is cricket or hockey India have national women team for every game. Indian women cricket team has won Asia Cup of 2004 and 2005 and made country proud. Some women sports icons of India are:

P.T. Usha (Athletics)

Kunjarani Devi (Weight lifting)

Diana Edulji (Cricket)

Sania Mirza (Tennis)

Karnam Malleshwari (Weight lifting)

Art and Entertainment

This area is full of Indian women. We have many names to boast of like M.S. Subbulakshmi, Indian Nightingale Lata Mangeshkar, Asha Bhosle as famous singers. Madhu Bala, Rekha, Aishwarya Rai as Bollywood queens. Today Indian woman is a painter, an actor, a singer, and a beauty queen.

Literature

Arundhati Roy, Anita Desai, Kiran Desai, Shobhaa De, Jhumpa

Lahiri are famous names in Indian literature. Not just in India now these women are recognized all over the world. Arundhati Roy has been awarded with the Booker Prize of 1997 for her work 'God of Small Things'. Kiran Desai has been given Booker Prize of 2006 and Jhumpa Lahiri got recognition in the form of Pulitzer prize.

Corporate Divas

Kiran Majumdar Shaw is the undisputed corporate queen of India. She is the richest Indian woman. Another names in this list include Vidya Mohan Chhabaria, Chairperson of Jumbo Group, Naina Lal Kidwai, Vice Chairperson and Managing Director of HSBC Securities and Capital Market, Sullaijja Firodia Motwani and Mallika Srinivasan.

Social Saints

The Indian saint of today's times Mother Teresa is the name which every Indian whether rich or poor is familiar with. Another important names working for the cause of people includes Aruna Roy who worked for the save RTI Campaign and Medha Patekar who is associated with Narmada Bachao Andolan.

Universal Queens

Kalpana Chawla, who was the member of Colombia Space Shuttle, which exploded on its way back, was the first Indian women astronaut who visited space station. And now following on her footsteps another women of Indian origin Sunita Williams has become the second one to be the member of International Space Station crew.

Indian women have mastered anything and everything which a woman can dream of. But she still has to go a long way to achieve equal status in the minds of Indian men.

Indian Culture vs Western Culture

Every country has its own set of rituals and cultures. Cultures differ from one country to another and from one region to another. No culture can be the same. This is also true with reference to Indian and western culture.

The Indian and western cultures differ in many aspects, such as, family relations, marital life, food, clothing, social life, and religious life.

Indian culture is considered to be one of the oldest cultures whereas western culture is considered to be modern.

When talking of family life, there is a great bond between family members in the Indian culture which cannot be seen in western culture. In Indian culture, one can come across joint families. When talking of western culture, however, they have only small family units. Another difference that can be seen is that western culture is more open. Though social mixing is very much common in western culture, these are not approved of in Indian culture. In dressing, the Indians dress in a very modest way and do not wear revealing dresses. Wearing revealing dresses, however, is quite common in the western culture.Though western people may become friends very soon, it cannot be taken as a commitment. If a person has to become committed to another, it may take some time in western culture. Indians are seen to become committed very soon.

In western culture, people have high esteem of their skills. They even openly admit their skills. Indians do not do so. They are somewhat shy and want some other person to boost their skills. Now, concerning the status of women, they are considered to be equal in western culture. However, in Indian culture, women do not share equal status with men. Nonetheless, at the same time, woman is held in high regard and is to be given respect and honor at all costs.

The two cultures are entirely different from one another, yet we can derive the best out of the both and create a pleasant living in the modern world.

Birth of Parallel Cinema in India

Cinema was born out of the impetus to represent the reality in a more convincing manner. An analysis of the earliest films clearly proves that. With the passage of time and the new technological achievements, cinema gradually metamorphosed itself into an entertainment medium. However cinema, like any other art forms, cannot be oblivious to the social changes that take place every day. It in fact mirrors the reality. Indian cinema is no exception. It has always reflected the social, political and economic changes throughout its history. In the 1970s, parallel cinema movement addressed this reality without any reservation. The birth of parallel cinema in India however was not a sudden phenomenon. The seed was sown much earlier.

1950s scenario

Soon after independence, India got its first constitution and the first five year plan also came into being. The winds of change in the political scenario gave Indian cinema a fresh lease of life with film makers questioning the post colonial issues like poverty, illiteracy and unjustified social system. Satyajit Ray with his neo-realist film 'Pather Panchali' (1955) heralded the beginning of a new genre of films, which many regard as the precursor of the parallel cinema. 'Aparajito' (1956) and 'Apur Sansar' (1959) further advanced Indian cinema towards what in the 1970s came to be known as the parallel cinema. Mrinal Sen, another noted Bengali filmmaker, also contributed immensely towards this goal. While these developments had been taking place in Bengal, a completely new breed of filmmakers like Shanta Ram and Shorab Modi in Bombay were carving niche for themselves with films that addressed social issues. These films were all chronicles of the social change that were taking place in the Indian society.

The Dismal 1960s

The questionings of these filmmakers during the 1950s turned sour in the 1960s. The discontent became even more pronounced soon after the death of Nehru and followed by the death of another prime minister, Lal Bahadur Sashtri. It was during this decade that India had fought two wars- one with Pakistan and another with China. The rising prices of the essential commodities, compounded further by the huge unemployment and drought, pushed the discontent of the Indians to the boiling point. Under these volatile circumstances parallel cinema was finally born in the 1970s.

1970s and the Beginning

1970 began on a dismal note. The Bangladesh war pushed further the already strained Indian economy to its limit. This decade also saw the suppression of civil liberties during the emergency and subsequently the constitutional break up. The parallel cinema or art cinema addressed these growing frustrations of the Indians by completely deviating itself from the feel good movies. Films made under this genre were completely de-glamorized with emphasis on stark reality and is characterized by the complete lack of visual opulence. Films like 'Interview', 'Ankur', 'Padatik' all exude anger, which was representative of the mood of the ordinary Indians.

Filmmakers like Mrinal Sen and Budhyadeb Das Gupta in West Bengal; G. Arvindan and Adoor Gopalakrishnan in Kerala; Shyam Benegal and Basu Chatterjee in Mumbai captured the prevalent mood of Indians through their films. The birth of Parallel cinema is also attributed to the various film schools that produced many educated filmmakers, who felt responsible for the cause of this new genre of cinema.

The parallel cinema of the 1970s however could not curb the supremacy of the Bollywood feel good movies. It nonetheless made the audience think for a while.

Fact vs. Truth

What is the clear difference between a fact and a truth? Well, if you look into most dictionaries, you will be amazed to find that the two words are actually very close in terms of their definitions. This is because the two terms are very much related. That's why you really can't blame people for recognizing both as similar terms.

Fact is basically something that exists, or is present in reality. Hence, these are things that can be seen visually, and these are the things that can actually be verified. Facts are objective matters rather than subjective ones. It is not just something that you believe, but rather these are more or less the things that can be observed empirically, or by the senses. So, facts can be seen and heard, as well as proven by the other senses.

Truth can be described as the true state of a certain matter, may it be a person, a place, a thing or an event. It is what a person has come to believe. If he believes that something is true, then it is true. It also answers the questions of what's really happening. In the technical sense, facts can answer certain 'why' questions, like 'where' or 'when', and even 'how', while truth answers the question 'why'. The question of 'how', and even 'what', are said to be answerable by either of the two.

In terms of permanence, a fact happens to be more permanent, and almost always seems to have no changes. It is more constant than truths. For example, when you say that the sun will always rise from the east and set in the west, you are telling a fact, but when you say that you are in Los Angeles, then that is a truth, at least for that exact moment. Several hours from that time you may have gone somewhere else, making your previous statement a fallacy. Thus, a truth is something that is not universal, it is more subjective, and depends on the current situation. That's why the truth's existence is said to be more temporary than that of facts.

■■■

Chapter 18

Letter Writing

Letter writing is also an art. Even though letters have transformed into e-mails and SMSs, the art still remains, only the medium has changed. Letters can be broadly classified into formal letters and informal letters. As the name suggests, formal letters include business letters, official letters, applications, complaints, letter to editors, letters written to people whom we want to convey certain important information. On the other hand, informal letters include personal letters, letters that are written to our friends and family. While formal letters follow certain format, one can be flexible while writing informal letters. Nonetheless, letter writing is a skill that needs to be honed over time with practice. It is a pleasurable task once you know the basic rules.

Let us understand a few ground rules while writing formal letters:

- You need to write your full name, address and date before you begin the letter.
- Address the person you are writing the letter to with correct name and designation.
- It is always advisable to start the letter with 'Respected Sir/

Madam' or 'Dear Sir/Madam' and then mention the name and the address.

- Before beginning to write the letter you must state the purpose of the letter in one line titled 'Subject'.
- Your letter should be very crisp giving out only that information which is required.
- You letter should state action/information required/ supplied or requesting action to be taken.
- While closing, do not forget to end your letter politely by using phrases like 'thanking you' and undersigning your letter using 'Yours faithfully/sincerely' (Name).

This is the basic structure of a letter. You can modify it according to the purpose for which it is written and the person to whom it is addressed. For example, if you are writing a letter for job application, then you may need to attach your resume along with the letter and also mention the same in it.

Now coming to informal letters, these are letters that do not have many rules. Since you are writing to your friends and family, you are free to choose your tone and content. One however needs to keep the following things in mind:

Write your full name and address even if it is an informal letter.

Divide your letter in small paragraphs.

Keep your writing simple.

Make a good choice of words especially if you are writing an apology letter or a letter to express your condolences in case of a death.

Most people close the letter with phrases like 'Yours affectionately/With love/All the best/Take care' etc.

Letter writing almost embarks you on a journey of words, then be it hand-written or typed, this is one activity that helps you communicate so beautifully.

Model Letters

These letters are useful for students who want to learn how to write particular types of letter in English. There is an application for a job, a letter to a newspaper and several complaint letters.

Complaint Letter from Business to Business

Dear Mr Sharma,

I recently received a letter from a Mr Rohit, a valued customer of ours. He purchased an Italian coffee table and four French dining-room chairs from us which your company delivered to his residence.

He has written to complain that the purchases arrived damaged. We pride ourselves in the quality of our products and would like an explanation as to how this mishap occurred. Even though the items are insured, our reputation is at stake.

I would be most grateful if you would reply as soon as possible so that this matter can be resolved to everyone's satisfaction.

Sincerely

Jatin Duggal

Customer Services Manager

Complaint Letter from a Business Customer to a Telephone Company

Dear Sir,

I am writing this letter to complain in the strongest terms about the poor service that I have received from your company.

We signed up to your telephone and internet service package two months ago because your advertising suggests that you are better than Telco. In addition, you promise to deal with problems quickly and efficiently, something that Telco were unable or unwilling to do. However, in the first month of service you managed to cause me to lose two days worth of business because of poor administration.

The main problem was that you failed to provide me with the correct telephone number, 9818 8747, that you had promised when I completed the contract. This phone number was an established business line which I had been using for the last three years.

Obviously this meant that my clients were unable to contact me and it cost me many hours of phone calls to resolve the matter with your support centre.

I would appreciate it if this situation could be resolved and a substantial rebate offered on my first three month's account.

I look forward to hearing from you soon.

Yours Faithfully

Ravi Shanka

Dear Sir,

As someone who has travelled throughout Asia on business and holiday I would like to give my opinion on its environmental impact. Having visited Indonesia, Thailand and Malaysia I understand that tourism can bring money to developing countries. However, this money often goes into the pockets of foreign investors, and only rarely benefits local people. Multinational hotel chains also have little regard for the surrounding wildlife when they build new resorts. This can cause many problems.

In view of these facts we, as tourists, can directly affect these countries in a positive way if we are thoughtful. When we visit these countries we can visit restaurants, bars and even hotels that are owned by local people. In addition, we can refuse to give luxury resorts our patronage and therefore prevent them from becoming even larger. Most importantly we should check that any tours or excursions we take have minimal effect on the natural surroundings.

Finally, we can even attempt to change the behaviour of other tourists by sharing our opinions.

If we follow these simple steps we can be sure that our pleasure is not causing any harm to people or places that we visit.

A Letter in Application for a Job

Dear Sir/Madam,

I am writing this letter to apply for the position of student assistant that I saw advertised on your website. I am interested in working in the teachers' resource library, or in the accommodation department.

I have recently graduated from the Delhi University and received high grades in both my English and Business Courses. In addition, we had to use all of the Microsoft Office programs in the preparation of our finished assignments, so I am able to do most things with computers.

Since I was 16 years old I have helped my father to run his small import-export business. I have been involved in helping a variety of clients and also the general administration of the business. In the past 2 years I have worked in the University library, helping teachers and students to find and use the resources there. This experience has given me the ability to deal with the needs of all types of people.

I have an outgoing, diligent personality and find that I enjoy the challenges of working in busy environments. In addition, my studies and experience have taught me to be accurate and efficient in organising my work so I would be a valuable addition to your school.

I look forward to hearing from you.

Yours faithfully

Parul Arora

Informal Letters

An informal Letter to Inform about Happenings

Hi Rekha,

It's been a while since we wrote, so I thought I'd drop you a line to bring you up to date with what's been happening here.

I suppose the most important thing is that Rita's job is more secure than we thought. At the beginning of the year, when she got the job, we thought it might only be for one semester, but we just found that she has a permanent contract of sorts. Obviously this is great, as it means we can relax a little. I still don't have what I really want work wise, but it will happen soon. You have to stay positive, don't you?

My parents are both fine, and I think they are really happy that we've moved back. For us, it's great to be so close to family again, an extra sense of comfort and security. We see my sister quite often as she's in London, although we're not that bothered about going into the city.

So, what about you these days? Are you still stuck in that old job? Since I've been having so much trouble getting a job I understand your reluctance to change. There's nothing worse than filling in endless application forms, with no idea of what it will lead to.

Anyway, I've got another form to fill in so I'll love you and leave you.

Regards

Chavi

An Informal Letter asking for a Favour

Hi Garima,

I'm writing this letter because I really need your help. You're the only person who knows me well enough to give me a reference for a course I want to do.

I saw an advert in a paper recently offering a free journalism course to successful applicants. I sent in an article I wrote for the student newspaper, you know, the one about legalising drugs? Anyway, they really liked it, but as there are only five places they want a reference as well. I haven't given them your name yet, as I expect this would be the first reference you've been asked to give. Is it OK if I send them your phone number? I think they want to phone so they can have a proper conversation with you and really check me out.

I know it's been a while but if you could do it it'd really help me out. I've got a new phone number, 09957 234 563, so you can get me on that, and my address is still the same.

Hope to hear from you soon.

Regards

Prashant

A Semi-formal E-mail in the form of a Report

Hi Dinesh,

Just getting back to you with a preliminary report on what we need to setup the multimedia suite in the library.

Firstly, I looked at cameras and other hardware that students will be borrowing.

As you know we're dealing with about 600 students on this site. In addition, there have been 6 tutors who have already been asking about digital cameras and digital video cameras, and they hadn't even heard about this project. Judging by the interest I don't think we should buy less than 4 of each, that way we can let a class take three at a time and still have one left over. We'll also need to ensure that the cameras are only lent out for a day at a time. I'm going to try to get some advice from other colleges about equipment which is both rugged and reliable enough to be borrowed by our students. We'll probably need to get a mini disc recorder as well, so students can record high quality sound.

The second area I looked at was the computer hardware we need.

Obviously, as we'll be dealing with video, image and audio files, we'll need as fast a processor as we can get, Mac or PC. We'll also need at least 512MB of RAM, but 1GB would actually be much better. For capturing video we'll need a 10,000 rpm hard drive as well, they're much faster than the old 7,200 rpm drives. They also need to be as large as we can afford. If we can get a deal it is probably better to get Macs, even if it'll take a little while for everyone to get used to them. I suppose that depends upon our preferred suppliers though. With a discount we should be able to get at least 3 workstations.

Finally we need to consider software.

We need to have a full range of media software, from print to video on at least one computer, preferably all three. It would be great if students had the opportunity to use whatever media was best for their particular project. I think it could be very interesting to help them use the internet as a vehicle for their opinions, and for demonstrating their skills.

So that's it for now. We're really looking at a budget of Rs 8,0 cr. for the hardware. We'll have to look at the licenses we already have for software to see if we'll need to spend much on that.

I'll get back to you when I have more info on the cameras.

Cheers

Vicky

Congratulation Letters

Hello,

It's always so wonderful when two people as nice as yourselves find happiness together. Your marriage is a big step in your lives and will bring you even closer together. While married life can have its ups and downs, I hope that, together, you will find every joy that you so deserve. May the coming years prove rich with laughter, love, and happiness.

Congratulations on your marriage!

Regards,

Kareena

This Letter Congratulates a Person or Couple on the Birth of a New Baby

Hello,

Congratulations on the birth of your baby! I know this must be a very special and exciting time for you. While having a child means that your life will never again be the same, I don't know a single parent who would trade being a mom or dad for anything.

I wish you and your new little <boy/girl> health and every happiness. Congratulations on this addition to your family.

Regards,

Aruna

Invitation Letters

Hello,

As I am sure you know, <name of person having the birthday> is having a birthday. It would mean so much to <him/her> if you would join us for a small celebration in <his/her> honour.

The party will be held at <location> on <date and time> Please RSVP by telephoning <host name> at <phone number>.

I know that <name of person having the birthday> will be absolutely thrilled to have you there. I hope you can make it and I look forward to seeing you then.

Regards,

Garima

Semi-formal Letters

Requesting Information

Dear Sir,

I should be grateful if you would send us your brochure and price list about your translation services.

We are currently developing our sales literature and web sites and are interested in translating these into five languages apart from English.

I look forward to hearing from you.

Yours faithfully

Bakul

Resume Covering Letter

Dear Madam

Director of Studies

I am interested in working as Director of Studies for your organisation. I am an EFL language instructor with nearly 10 years' experience to offer you. I enclose my resume as a first step in exploring the possibilities of employment with Interplay Languages.

My most recent experience was implementing English Through Drama workshops for use with corporate clients. I was responsible for the overall pedagogical content, including the student coursebook. In addition, I developed the first draft of the teacher's handbook.

As Director of Studies with your organisation, I would bring a focus on quality and effectiveness to your syllabus design. Furthermore, I work well with others, and I am experienced in course planning.

I would appreciate your keeping this enquiry confidential. I will call you in a few days to arrange an interview at a time convenient to you. Thank you for your consideration.

Yours faithfully

Fatima

Letter of Reference

To Whom It May Concern:

Reference for Mr Varun Mogga

Varun Mogga joined the A.N.Y. Company in July 1998.

Varun is professional and efficient in his approach to work and very well-liked by his colleagues and executive clients. He is well-presented and able to work both independently and as part of a team.

His contribution to all areas of company activity in which he has been involved have been much appreciated.

I believe that Varun will make a valuable addition to any organisation that he may join. We deeply regret his decision to move on and I recommend him without hesitation.

I would gladly answer any request for further information.

Sincerely,

Paras Manchanda

Managing Director

Resignation Letter

Dear Mrs. Duggal,

I am writing to provide formal notice of my resignation from Fielders Pharmacy. My last day will be March 14th, 2011.

I trust that two weeks is sufficient notice for you to find a replacement for my position. I would be pleased to help train the individual you choose to take my place.

Thank you for employing me for the past three years. My experience as clerk, supervisor, and floor manager has been very positive and I'm confident that I will use many of the skills I have learned at Fielders in the future.

If you have any concerns, please contact me at my personal email address.

All the best,

Ana D'Souza

Payment Request

Dear Mr. Dhruv

Our records show that you have an outstanding balance dating back to December 2010. Your December invoice was for Rs. 20,000 and we have yet to receive this payment. Please find a copy of the invoice enclosed.

If this amount has already been paid, please disregard this notice. Otherwise, please forward us the amount owed in full by March 31, 2011. As our contract indicates, we begin charging 5% interest for any outstanding balances after 30 days.

Thank you in advance for your cooperation. We hope to continue doing business with you in the future.

Sincerely,

Maria

Accountant

Enclosure: Invoice #223

Condolence letter

Dear Robert

I would like to express my sincere condolences on the recent passing of your father. Pamela and the children also send their thoughts and prayers to you and your family at this difficult time.

Although I didn't know your dad that well, on the half dozen or so occasions that I spent time in his company over the years, I did come to realise his great kindness and compassion towards those less fortunate than him. And I do know that he was very highly respected throughout this community and profession, and his good works changed the lives of many.

You were truly fortunate to have such a man as a model in your life.

As you know, it was not that long ago that my own father passed away, so I have some idea of what you and your family are going through. No comfort is quite enough to replace the loss.

Please pass my deepest sympathies on to your mother, and brother, and sister, and to all of your father's grandchildren.

Very sincerely,

Sumit

■■■

Chapter 19

Story Writing

Since prehistoric times, when tales were told around fires and painted on cave walls, stories have been an essential part of our human experience. But what exactly is a story – and how can you write a great one?

A story is simply a tale of events that are linked by cause and effect. It can be true or it can be a work of fiction. We expect stories to have a beginning, middle and end; they involve at least two characters, and some events take place.

The Short Story

The Novel

The Life Story (Biography or Autobiography)

Three Types of Story

1. Short Stories

Short stories are published in magazines, newspapers and book anthologies. Short stories need:

A small cast of characters, with one main character.

A compact time frame, with the story taking place over the course of a few days or weeks

A single plot without subplots, though longer short stories may have a subplot.

The majority of writing competitions are for complete short stories, rather than novels or novel excerpts.

How to Write a Great Short Story?

Like any story, your short story needs to have a beginning, middle and end:

The beginning is where we're introduced to the characters, especially the main character and his/her problem.

The middle is where the action and plot develops. The main character will face difficulties such as opposition from other people or a challenging environment.

The end is where the main character triumphs over his/her biggest challenge (or fails, in the case of a tragedy). The resolution should be satisfying and conclusive for the reader.

2. Novels

Novels and short stories share similar structural features, but novels give the author a much wider scope. A novel might have:

More than one main character (though attempt this with caution!)

A large cast of characters

A long time frame – potentially covering several centuries and several generations

Multiple subplots.

How to Write a Novel?

A novel is a much bigger undertaking than a short story. Even if you are able to write short stories without much planning, you'll need to plan out your novel in advance. There are a number of ways to do this, but whichever you choose, ensure:

You have enough plot to meet your word count target.

Your main character (protagonist) is sympathetic – readers of short stories will put up with a dull or unlikeable character, but novel readers are stuck with the character's viewpoint for much longer. As the writer, you'll need to be able to become your characters.

You have an escalation of events throughout the plot. Things need to get worse and worse for your characters, until they finally overcome their problems or enemies.

3. Life Stories

A life story is a true story – though it shares features with fictional stories. Life stories are either 'biography' (when you write about someone else) or 'autobiography' (when you write about yourself).

Most biographies and autobiographies are book length, similar to a novel.

How to write a Life Story?

A life story needs to be engaging and interesting for the reader. Don't include boring details just because they're 'true' – the reader doesn't need to know everything that happened. In many cases, details of childhood or dull years can be summarised – or told through a few vividly-drawn incidents.

You will need to be careful when writing a biography or autobiography to:

Structure your piece as a story, focusing on interesting events and incidents.

Show the personality of the subject (yourself or the person you're writing about), and making sure the reader will find them at least partly likeable.

Be conscious of the other people involved – try to be sensitive to how they might feel (and avoid getting sued for libel – make sure you're certain of your facts). There is often a fine line between life writing and fiction. If you are writing the story of your life, you will need to make decisions about whether you will alter or make up lines of dialogue, for instance.

General Story Writing Tips

Whatever type of story or stories you're writing, and however experienced you are, there's always room for improvement...

- Share Your Story Writing Efforts

It's hard to write in isolation, and sharing your work with other writers is a great way to get feedback and suggestions. Look for a local writers' circle, or join an online forum. You want to find somewhere that's supportive but where people aren't afraid to offer advice about things that aren't working in your story.

- Keep Learning

Writing is a craft that you can learn, like any other. There are hundreds of books on all aspects of writing, from the nuts and bolts of grammar and punctuation to writing in specific genres.

- Keep Practicing

As well as learning about writing, you need to practice. That means writing regularly – ideally daily. As you write more, your stories will get better – your characters are more 'real', your plots are convincing, and your endings are deeply satisfying to readers. You'll also find that writing itself becomes easier: you'll spend less time struggling to find the right words, and more time enjoying seeing the story spill from your fingers.

- Always Revise

All authors need to revise their work. Your first draft might have a lot of problems – inconsistent characterization, scenes which don't really fit, holes in the plot, incorrect pacing or tension. Don't worry if this is the case: most published authors have to extensively rewrite their first drafts too. Always allow time to revise your story, and if possible, do several rewrites. Most authors recommend letting your story sit unread for a few days or weeks when you complete a draft, so that you can come to it with fresh eyes.

Short Stories

Puppies for Sale

A farmer had some puppies he needed to sell. He painted a sign advertising the pups and set about Nailing it to a post on the edge of his yard. As he was driving the last nail into the post, he felt a tug on his overalls. He looked down into the eyes of a little boy.

'Mister,' he said, 'I want to buy one of your puppies.'

'Well,' said the farmer, as he rubbed the sweat off the back of his neck, 'these puppies come from fine parents and cost a good deal of money.'

The boy dropped his head for a moment. Then reaching deep into his pocket, he pulled out a handful of change and held it up to the farmer. 'I've got Rs 2000. Is that enough to take a look?'

'Sure,' said the farmer.

And with that he let out a whistle, 'Here, Dolly!' he called.

Out from the doghouse and down the ramp ran Dolly followed by four little balls of fur. The little boy pressed his face against the chain link fence. His eyes danced with delight.

As the dogs made their way to the fence, the little boy noticed something else stirring inside the doghouse. Slowly another little ball appeared; this One noticeably smaller. Down the ramp it slid. Then in a somewhat awkward manner the little pup began hobbling toward the others, doing its best to catch up....

'I want that one,' the little boy said, pointing to the runt.

The farmer knelt down at the boy's side and said, 'Son, you don't want that puppy. He will never be able to run and play with you like these other dogs would.'

With that the little boy stepped back from the fence, reached down, and began rolling up one leg of his trousers. In doing so he revealed a steel brace running down both sides of his leg attaching itself To a specially made shoe. Looking back up at the farmer, he said, 'You see sir, I don't run too well myself, and he will need Someone who understands.' The world is full of people who need someone who understands.

Wait for the Brick

A young and successful executive was travelling down a neighbourhood street, going a bit too fast in his new Jaguar. He was watching for kids darting out from between parked cars and slowed down when he thought he saw something. As his car passed, no children appeared. Instead, a brick smashed into the Jag's side door! He slammed on the brakes and drove the Jag back to the spot where the brick had been thrown. The angry driver then jumped out of the car, grabbed the nearest kid and pushed him up against a parked car, shouting, 'What was that all about and who are you? Just what the heck are you doing? That's a new car and that brick you threw is going to cost a lot of money. Why did you do it?'

The young boy was apologetic. 'Please mister ... please, I'm sorry... I didn't know what else to do,' he pleaded.

'I threw the brick because no one else would stop...'

With tears dripping down his face and off his chin, the youth pointed to a spot just around a parked car.

'It's my brother,' he said.

'He rolled off the curb and fell out of his wheelchair and I can't lift him up.'

Now sobbing, the boy asked the stunned executive, 'Would you please help me get him back into his wheelchair? He's hurt and he's too heavy for me.'

Moved beyond words, the driver tried to swallow the rapidly swelling lump in his throat.

He hurriedly lifted the handicapped boy back into the wheelchair, then took out his fancy handkerchief and dabbed at the fresh scrapes and cuts. A quick look told him everything was going to be okay.

'Thank you and may God bless you,' the grateful child told the stranger.

Too shook up for words, the man simply watched the little boy push his wheelchair-bound brother down the sidewalk toward their home. It was a long, slow walk back to the Jaguar. The damage was very noticeable, but the driver never bothered to repair the dented side door. He kept the dent there to remind him of this message: Don't go through life so fast that someone has to throw a brick at you to get your attention!

God whispers in our souls and speaks to our hearts. Sometimes when we don't have time to listen, He has to throw a brick at us.

It's our choice: Listen to the whisper ... or wait for the brick!

The Wooden Bowl

A frail old man went to live with his son, daughter-in-law, and a four-year old grandson. The old man's hands trembled, his eyesight was blurred, and his steps faltered. The family ate together nightly at the dinner table.

But the elderly grandfather's shaky hands and failing sight made eating rather difficult. Peas rolled off his spoon onto the floor. When he grasped the glass, often milk spilled on the tablecloth. The son and daughter-in-law became irritated with the mess.

'We must do something about grandfather,' said the son. 'I've had enough of his spilled milk, noisy eating, and food on the floor.'

So, the husband and wife set a small table in the corner. There, grandfather ate alone while the rest of the family enjoyed dinner at the dinner table. Since grandfather had broken a dish or two, his food was served in a wooden bowl. Sometimes when the family glanced in grandfather's direction, he had a tear in his eye as he ate alone. Still, the only words the couple had for him were sharp admonitions when he dropped a fork or spilled food. The four-year-old watched it all in silence.

One evening, before supper, the father noticed his son playing with wood scraps on the floor. He asked the child sweetly, 'What are you making?' Just as sweetly, the boy responded, 'Oh, I am making a little bowl for you and mama to eat your food from when I grow up.'

Saying this, the four-year-old smiled and went back to work. The words so struck the parents that they were speechless. Then tears started to stream down their cheeks. Though no word was spoken, both knew what must be done. That evening the husband took grandfather's hand and gently led him back to the family table.

For the remainder of his days he ate every meal with the family. And for some reason, neither husband nor wife seemed to care any longer when a fork was dropped, milk spilled, or the tablecloth soiled. Children are remarkably perceptive. Their eyes ever observe, their ears ever listen, and their minds ever process the messages they absorb. If they see us patiently provide a happy home atmosphere for family members, they will imitate that attitude for the rest of their lives. The wise parent realises that every day that building blocks are being laid for the child's future.

Let us all be wise builders and role models. Take care of yourself, ... and those you love, ... today, and everyday!

Hopes and Dreams

Once there were three trees on a hill in the woods. They were discussing their hopes and dreams when the first tree said, 'Someday I hope to be a treasure chest. I could be filled with gold, silver and precious gems. I could be decorated with intricate carving and everyone would see the beauty.'

Then the second tree said, 'Someday I will be a mighty ship. I will take kings and queens across the waters and sail to the corners of the world. Everyone will feel safe in me because of the strength of my hull.'

Finally the third tree said, 'I want to grow to be the tallest and straightest tree in the forest. People will see me on top of the hill and look up to my branches, and think of the heavens and God and how close to them I am reaching. I will be the greatest tree of all time and people will always remember me.'

After a few years of praying that their dreams would come true, a group of woodsmen came upon the trees. When one came to the first tree he said, 'This looks like a strong tree, I think I should be able to sell the wood to a carpenter' ... and he began cutting it down. The tree was happy, because he knew that the carpenter would make him into a treasure chest.

At the second tree a woodsman said, 'This looks like a strong tree, I should be able to sell it to the shipyard.' The second tree was happy because he knew he was on his way to becoming a mighty ship.

When the woodsmen came upon the third tree, the tree was frightened because he knew that if they cut him down his dreams would not come true. One of the woodsmen said, 'I don't need anything special from my tree so I'll take this one', and he cut it down.

When the first tree arrived at the carpenters, he was made into a feed box for animals. He was then placed in a barn and filled with hay. This was not at all what he had prayed for. The second tree was cut and made into a small fishing boat. His dreams of being a mighty ship and carrying kings had come to an end. The third tree was cut into large pieces and left alone in the dark. The years went by, and the trees forgot about their dreams.

Then one day, a man and woman came to the barn. She gave birth and they placed the baby in the hay in the feed box that was made from the first tree. The man wished that he could have made a crib for the baby, but this manager would have to do. The tree could feel the importance of this event and knew that it had held the greatest treasure of all time.

Years later, a group of men got in the fishing boat made from the second tree. One of them was tired and went to sleep. While they were out on the water, a great storm arose and the tree didn't think it was strong enough to keep the men safe. The men woke the sleeping man, and he stood and said 'Peace' and the storm stopped. At this time, the tree knew that it had carried the King of Kings in its boat.

Finally, someone came and got the third tree. It was carried through the streets as the people mocked the man who was carrying it. When they came to a stop, the man was nailed to the tree and raised in the air to die at the top of a hill.

When Sunday came, the tree came to realise that it was strong enough to stand at the top of the hill and be as close to God as was possible, because Jesus had been crucified on it.

The moral of this story is that when things don't seem to be going your way, always know that God has a plan for you. If you place your trust in Him, He will give you great gifts. Each of the trees got what they wanted, just not in the way they had imagined. We don't always know what God's plans are for us. We just know that His ways are not our ways, but His ways are always best.

The Mountain Story

'A son and his father were walking on the mountains.

Suddenly, his son falls, hurts himself and screams, 'AAAhhhhhhhhhhh!!!'

To his surprise, he hears the voice repeating, somewhere in the mountain: 'AAAhhhhhhhhhhh!!!'

Curious, he yells, 'Who are you?'

He receives the answer, 'Who are you?'

And then he screams to the mountain, 'I admire you!'

The voice answers, 'I admire you!'

Angered at the response, he screams, 'Coward!'

He receives the answer, 'Coward!'

He looks to his father and asks, 'What's going on?'

The father smiles and says, 'My son, pay attention.'

Again the man screams, 'You are a champion!'

The voice answers, 'You are a champion!'

The boy is surprised, but does not understand.

Then the father explains, 'People call this ECHO, but really this is LIFE.

It gives you back everything you say or do.

Our life is simply a reflection of our actions.

If you want more love in the world, create more love in your heart.

If you want more competence in your team, improve your competence.

This relationship applies to everything, in all aspects of life;

Life will give you back everything you have given to it.

Your life is not a coincidence. It's a reflection of you!

Building Your House

An elderly carpenter was ready to retire. He told his employer-contractor of his plans to leave the house-building business to live a more leisurely life with his wife and enjoy his extended family. He would miss the paycheck each week, but he wanted to retire. They could get by.

The contractor was sorry to see his good worker go and asked if he could build just one more house as a personal favour. The carpenter said yes, but over time it was easy to see that his heart was not in his work. He resorted to shoddy workmanship and used inferior materials. It was an unfortunate way to end a dedicated career.

When the carpenter finished his work, his employer came to inspect the house. Then he handed the front-door key to the carpenter and said, 'This is your house... my gift to you.'

The carpenter was shocked!

What a shame! If he had only known he was building his own house, he would have done it all so differently.

So it is with us. We build our lives, a day at a time, often putting less than our best into the building. Then, with a shock, we realise we have to live in the house we have built. If we could do it over, we would do it much differently.

But, you cannot go back. You are the carpenter, and every day you hammer a nail, place a board, or erect a wall. Someone once said, 'Life is a do-it-yourself project.' Your attitude, and the choices you make today, help build the 'house' you will live in tomorrow. Therefore, Build wisely.

The Rose Within

A certain man planted a rose and watered it faithfully and before it blossomed, he examined it.

He saw the bud that would soon blossom, but noticed thorns upon the stem and he thought, 'How can any beautiful flower come from a plant burdened with so many sharp thorns? Saddened by this thought, he neglected to water the rose, and just before it was ready to bloom... it died.

So it is with many people. Within every soul there is a rose. The God-like qualities planted in us at birth, grow amid the thorns of our faults. Many of us look at ourselves and see only the thorns, the defects.

We despair, thinking that nothing good can possibly come from us. We neglect to water the good within us, and eventually it dies. We never realise our potential.

Some people do not see the rose within themselves; someone else must show it to them. One of the greatest gifts a person can possess is to be able to reach past the thorns of another, and find the rose within them.

This is one of the characteristic of love... to look at a person, know their true faults and accepting that person into your life... all the while recognising the nobility in their soul. Help others to realize they can overcome their faults. If we show them the 'rose' within themselves, they will conquer their thorns. Only then will they blossom many times over.

One Life Gone!!!

A mother was devastated, she was howling with pain, yelling all she could in that dark and dingy corner of her four by four kholi. There was nobody to hear her yell and not a soul to pacify her, because outside her shack is a long winding lonely road. There was no existence of mankind for miles and miles ahead. The wind was at rest, the leaves didn't rustle and no resonance of a barking dog, silence filled the air. Loneliness was already killing her, but no one knows what made her cry?

Losing something you love with all your heart isn't really the grief you can ever overcome. Radha lost her baby. Her only means to live. She saw her child getting crushed under a car in front of her own eyes. Blood was all over and the accident was terrible. One lonely night, she was walking down the street to get a breath of fresh air with her child cuddled tight in her arms. She walked a long time still she saw the face of mankind (in the evilest form).

The whole time she walked with her child in her arms the only thing that worried her was Aryans (her son's) future. What kind of a person will he be? Will he make me proud? How much light is life going to bring in his existence? She was imagining and feeling every day of the Childs growth, and what she had in store for him. But who knows what's in store for us tomorrow, life can change in the splits of a second. Talk about destiny, all those dreams hopes and expectations were snatched away from her in an instant. Her smiles were frowns and her faith just crumbled, like a dead soul in a living, rather breathing body.

This is how it happened.... On that abandoned road, were a few streetlights barely sufficient? There was this one light that was visible from a distance, but as it came closer it got brighter and brighter. That light changed Radha's life into darkness forever. A speeding car came down that road, as if the driver had jammed the accelerator, cutting across the wind. He came at a speed of 110 kmph throwing beer bottles out of his half open window. He was definitely drunk, the speed took everything in its path. Just then, there was a loud cry, and silence set in again. The cry of a baby and no sight of a child.

Ironically the mother wasn't hurt, not a scratch on her body, not a bruise on her arm. She opened her eyes and didn't see Aryan, her vision was blur. After a few minutes when her sight cleared up she looked all over frantically for her baby, but alas! There was nothing. Just then she noticed something about ten feet away it was blood draining into the gutter's, and pieces of minced flesh, laying there saying so much without saying anything at all. The blood of her baby, the child who hadn't even seen life.

He paid the price for another man's folly. The same little child whose future was just being planned.

Simple, don't drink and drive. You could take a life, but kill a number of people.

Parable of the Pencil

The Pencil Maker took the pencil aside, just before putting him into the box.

'There are 5 things you need to know,' he told the pencil, 'Before I send you out into the world. Always remember them and never forget, and you will become the best pencil you can be.'

'One: You will be able to do many great things, but only if you allow yourself to be held in Someone's hand.'

'Two: You will experience a painful sharpening from time to time, but you'll need it to become a better pencil.'

'Three: You will be able to correct any mistakes you might make.'

'Four: The most important part of you will always be what's inside.'

'And Five: On every surface you are used on, you must leave your mark. No matter what the condition, you must continue to write.'

The pencil understood and promised to remember, and went into the box with purpose in its heart.

Now replacing the place of the pencil with you. Always remember them and never forget, and you will become the best person you can be.

One: You will be able to do many great things, but only if you allow yourself to be held in God's hand. And allow other human beings to access you for the many gifts you possess.

Two: You will experience a painful sharpening from time

to time, by going through various problems in life, but you'll need it to become a stronger person.

Three: You will be able to correct any mistakes you might make.

Four: The most important part of you will always be what's on the inside.

And Five: On every surface you walk through, you must leave your mark. No matter what the situation, you must continue to do your duties.

Allow this parable on the pencil to encourage you to know that you are a special person and only you can fulfil the purpose to which you were born to accomplish.

Never allow yourself to get discouraged and think that your life is insignificant and cannot make a change.

Praying Hands

Back in the fifteenth century, in a tiny village near Nuremberg, lived a family with eighteen children. Eighteen! In order merely to keep food on the table for this mob, the father and head of the household, a goldsmith by profession, worked almost eighteen hours a day at his trade and any other paying chore he could find in the neighbourhood. Despite their seemingly hopeless condition, two of Albrecht Durer the Elder's children had a dream. They both wanted to pursue their talent for art, but they knew full well that their father would never be financially able to send either of them to Nuremberg to study at the Academy.

After many long discussions at night in their crowded bed, the two boys finally worked out a pact. They would toss a coin. The loser would go down into the nearby mines and, with his earnings, support his brother while he attended the academy. Then, when that brother who won the toss completed his studies, in four years, he would support the other brother at the academy, either with sales of his artwork or, if necessary, also by labouring in the mines.

They tossed a coin on a Sunday morning after church. Albrecht Durer won the toss and went off to Nuremberg. Albert went down into the dangerous mines and, for the next four years, financed his brother, whose work at the academy was almost an immediate sensation.

Albrecht's etchings, his woodcuts, and his oils were far better than those of most of his professors, and by the time he graduated, he was beginning to earn considerable fees for his commissioned works.

When the young artist returned to his village, the Durer family held a festive dinner on their lawn to celebrate Albrecht's triumphant homecoming. After a long and memorable meal, punctuated with music and laughter, Albrecht rose from his honoured position at the head of the table to drink a toast to his beloved brother for the years of sacrifice that had enabled Albrecht to fulfil his ambition.

His closing words were, 'And now, Albert, blessed brother of mine, now it is your turn. Now you can go to Nuremberg to pursue your dream, and I will take care of you.'

All heads turned in eager expectation to the far end of the table where Albert sat, tears streaming down his pale face, shaking his lowered head from side to side while he sobbed and repeated, over and over, 'No ...no ...no ...no.'

Finally, Albert rose and wiped the tears from his cheeks. He glanced down the long table at the faces he loved, and then, holding his hands close to his right cheek, he said softly, 'No, brother. I cannot go to Nuremberg.

It is too late for me. Look ... look what four years in the mines have done to my hands! The bones in every finger have been smashed at least once, and lately I have been suffering from arthritis so badly in my right hand that I cannot even hold a glass to return your toast, much less make delicate lines on parchment or canvas with a pen or a brush. No, brother ...for me it is too late.'

More than 450 years have passed. By now, Albrecht Durer's hundreds of masterful portraits, pen and silver-point sketches, water colours, charcoals, woodcuts, and copper engravings hang in every great museum in the world, but the odds are great that you, like most people, are familiar with only one of Albrecht Durer's works. More than merely being familiar with it, you very well may have a reproduction hanging in your home or office.

One day, to pay homage to Albert for all that he had sacrificed, Albrecht Durer painstakingly drew his brother's abused hands with palms together and thin fingers stretched skyward. He called his powerful drawing simply 'Hands,' but the entire world almost immediately opened their hearts to his great masterpiece and renamed his tribute of love 'The Praying Hands.'

The next time you see a copy of that touching creation, take a second look. Let it be your reminder, if you still need one, that no one - no one - - ever makes it alone!

Sand and Stone

A story tells that two friends were walking through the desert. During some point of the journey they had an argument, and one friend slapped the other one on the face. The one who got slapped was hurt, but without saying anything, wrote in the sand, 'TODAY MY BEST FRIEND SLAPPED ME ON THE FACE.'

They kept on walking until they found an oasis, where they decided to take a bath. The one, who had been slapped, got stuck in the mire and started drowning, but the friend saved him.

After the friend recovered from the near drowning, he wrote on a stone: 'TODAY MY BEST FRIEND SAVED MY LIFE.'

The friend who had slapped and saved his best friend asked him, 'After I hurt you, you wrote in the sand and now, you write on a stone, why?'

The other friend replied: 'When someone hurts us, we should write it down in sand where winds of forgiveness can erase it away. But, when someone does something good for us, we must engrave it in stone where no wind can ever erase it.'

LEARN TO WRITE YOUR HURTS IN THE SAND, AND TO CARVE YOUR BENEFITS IN STONE

The Day Dreaming Priest

Once upon a time there lived a priest. He was extremely lazy and poor at the same time. He did not want to do any hard work but used to dream of being rich one day. He got his food by begging for alms. One morning, he got a pot of milk as part of the alms. He was extremely delighted and went home with the pot of milk. He boiled the milk, drank some of it and put the remaining milk in a pot. He added slight curds in the pot for converting the milk to curd. He then lay down to sleep.

Soon he started imagining about the pot of curd while he lay asleep. He dreamt that if he could become rich somehow all his miseries would be gone. His thoughts turned to the pot of milk he had set to form curd. He dreamt on; "By morning the pot of milk would set, it would be converted to curd. I would churn the curd and make butter from it. I would heat the butter and make ghee out of it. I will then go to that market and sell that ghee, and make some money. With that money, I will buy a hen. The hen will lay many eggs which will hatch and there will be many chickens. These chickens will in turn lay hundreds of eggs and I will soon have a poultry farm of my own." He kept on imagining.

"I will sell all the hens of my poultry and buy some cows, and open a milk dairy. All the town people will buy milk from me. I will be very rich and soon I shall buy jewels. The king will buy all the jewels from me. I will be so rich that I will be able to marry an exceptionally beautiful girl from a rich family. Soon, I will have a handsome son. If he does any mischief I will be very angry and to teach him a lesson, I will hit him with a big stick." During this dream, he involuntarily picked up the stick next to his bed and thinking that he was beating his son, raised the stick and hit the pot. The pot of milk broke and he awoke from his day dream.

So remember children, there is no substitute for hard work. Dreams cannot be fulfilled without hard work.

Mahabharat and Delhi Sultan's Wish

Tenali Ramakrishna was a court-poet of the Vijaya Nagar Empire in the 16th century. He was popular all over India for his wisdom and stories. His stories ruled parts of the sub-continent with Delhi as their capital for over two centuries. Few of the Mohammedan rulers maintained patience towards Hindu rituals and maintained communal harmony encouraging Hindu scholars and prophets.

Delhi was in Adil Shah's rule concurrently while Sri Krishna Deva Rayalu was ruling Vijaya Nagar. A war broke out between the two kingdoms for supremacy over one another. At one stage, both the rulers felt there was a need to establish peace in the region. Adil Shah invited Rayalu to Delhi for finalizing the peace treaty.

Hoping to utilise the opportunity to establish a cordial relation between the two empires, Rayalu headed for Delhi with a big team comprising of poets, dancers, scholars and others. At Delhi, Adil Shah gave red carpet welcome to Rayalu.

During the pleasant rounds of discussions, Adil Shah urged the scholars and poets from the Rayalu band to recite some sequences from the epic Mahabharat.

The visitors recited several sequences to please the Delhi Sultan. It was then that trouble shot up for the Vijaya Nagar ruler. Adil Shah expressed his wish and requested Rayalu to make his men rewrite the Mahabharat portraying him and his friends as Pandavas and his rivals as Kauravas. The total visiting team was shocked to hear the Sultan. They somehow managed to close the day's meeting immediately.

Rayalu was worried about the development. He called for an emergency meeting with the learned persons of his team. In the meeting, he sought suggestions from them to avert the problem. Everyone started scratching their heads to find an amicable solution. None could come out with any concrete proposal. After watching all this, suddenly Ramalinga raised and put his proposal before Rayalu.

He said, "My Lord! I think there is not much for you or us to get so much worried and burdened about the Delhi Sultan's wish about Mahabharat. You please leave the problem onto my shoulders and have a relaxed sleep. I will solve the problem without any problem." The King Rayalu had his own doubts about the safety of the kingdom and its people.

"Ramalinga..." Rayalu said, "...I am aware that you are a genius. However, it is not a common situation. Dealing with the Delhi Sultan is not an easy job. It is similar to fete on the edge of a sword. You should be very careful!" He was worried that if the problem was not dealt properly, there was a chance that Delhi Sultan might declare a war on Vijaya Nagar.

Ramalinga was stiff to his argument and assured everyone to leave the matter to him. Next morning, the court was packed with both the rulers and their henchmen. Adil Shah recalled his wish about re-composing of the Mahabharat. Ramalinga rose from his seat and saluted the Sultan. He started, "Huzoor! All of our poets are into the job assigned by your majesty's wish. However, every one of us is stuck at one specific issue. It is not proper for us to discuss the subject in the court. If you can kindly permit me, I wish to present the poking issue before you in private."

Adil Shah thought that there should really be some problem and consented for the one-on-one meeting with Ramalinga in a separate room. Ramalinga folding hands and presenting all respects to the Sultan in his words started, "Your Highness! You are the king of kings! It was our pleasure to know about your inclination about our epics like Mahabharat. The poets and scholars started re-composing the whole epic, in accordance to your majesty's wish. You are being portrayed as Dharmaraja, eldest of Pandavas and your friends as Bheema, Arjuna, Nakula and Sahadeva."

Ramalinga paused a second and continued, "This is where we had to scratch our brains..." However he was not forth coming with the problem. Adil Shah waited and when it was clear that he has to get it out of Ramalinga he ordered, "What is the problem? Tell me clearly and quickly."

"You are aware Huzoor! That Pandavas are five. All the five were married to Draupadi and were sharing her equally..." Ramalinga stressed, "We are unable to portray your image as Dharmaraja in this regard, thinking about the prestige of the King of Kings...."

Long before Ramalinga could complete, Adil Shah hastened to say, "Stop this nonsense now. I cannot take this anymore. Stop rewriting Mahabharat immediately. I can never accept this."

Ramalinga tried to say... "Huzoor! We started to work as per your wish...now, how can we turn away from the word given to you by us...we..."

"Look Poet!" Adil Shah raised his voice, "you should drop the Mahabharat topic as of now if you wish the friendship and co-operation between the two kingdoms to last long. Is that clear" and walked off the room.

Ramalinga bubbling with joy returned to his King Rayalu and his bandwagon of delegation and explained the whole sequence. Everyone including Rayalu appreciated the sharp intelligence and presence of mind Ramalinga had in solving the toughest problem just like that!

Crows and the Serpent

Long time ago, there lived a crow couple who had built a nest on top of a tree. But unfortunately the tree was inhabited by a serpent at its bottom. So the serpent used to crawl up the tree and eat all the eggs that the lady crow used to lay. The crow couple was deeply grieved. When this happened time after time, they decided that the serpent has to be get rid off by a plan.

So, the crow approached his friend jackal and asked for a plan. The jackal then told him to go and fetch a costly thing from the palace of the king and throw it in the burrow of the snake. The crow went to palace, and stole a necklace of the queen while she was bathing. The guards of the palace ran after it. The crow then dropped the necklace in the burrow of the snake beneath the tree.

The guards, on reaching the bottom of the tree, found the necklace guarded by the serpent. Seeing this, they killed the serpent and recovered the necklace. The crow family was now happy that their eggs were safe now.

The Gold Giving Serpent

Long time ago, there lived a poor brahman. He used to work hard on the fields but all his efforts did not bear fruit. One day, he found an anthill on his field and found a serpent there. Thinking that he had not paid respect to the guardian deity of his field, he procured milk and started feeding the anthill with milk from that day. One day, he found a gold coin in the plate. After that, he used to get a gold coin everyday he fed the serpent with milk.

Then one day he had to go to the town and asked his son to look after the serpent by feeding him the milk. The son was greedy and he thought, "This anthill must be full of gold coins. I must get all the coins today." Thinking this, he stuck the serpent. Unluckily the serpent did not die and it attacked the boy and he died.

The moral of the story is that excess greed is harmful.

Eagles in a Storm

An eagle knows when a storm is approaching. Sensing it, the eagle will fly to some high spot and wait for the winds to come. When the storm hits, it sets its wings so that the wind will pick it up and lift it above the storm. While the storm rages below, the eagle is soaring above it.

The eagle does not escape the storm. It simply uses the storm to lift it higher. It rises on the winds that bring the storm.

When the storms of life come upon us - and all of us will experience them - we can rise above them by setting our minds and our belief toward God. The storms do not have to overcome us. We can allow God's power to lift us above them.

God enables us to ride the winds of the storm that bring sickness, tragedy, failure and disappointment in our lives. We can soar above the storm.

Remember, it is not the burdens of life that weigh us down; it is how we handle them.

Bambi

This story takes place a very long time ago, deep in the forest.

In a part of the forest, a baby deer was born (a baby deer is called a 'fawn') Oh my, there was so much excitement that day. All the animals wanted to come and see the new fawn. Do you know why? It is because this was a special fawn. He was a young Prince. That means that one day, this tiny baby, would be all grown up and become the leader of all the deer in the forest. The birds sang the happiest song. 'Drip drip drop little April showers!' What a beautiful, beautiful spring day it was!

Thumper, a cute little rabbit, asked mama deer what she was going to call her baby. She smiled and looked down at her son and then at Thumper. "I am going to call him Bambi," she said. Thumper stood there for a moment, thumping his foot. "That' a funny name", he said at last. Thumper's mommy scolded him gently. "Thumper", she said, "What did your father tell you this morning?" Thumper hung his head down, just a bit and replied, "If you can't say something nice, don't say anything at all!" And you know that is really what we should all remember. We should always remember to say nice things about each other.

It was a happy time for Bambi. He soon learned to do many things. Thumper was his best friend. They did all kinds of fun stuff together. In no time at all, Bambi was standing up. Oh yes he was really wobbly at first. Thumper just had to laugh at him. But that was ok because it was a nice kind of laughter, and Bambi did not mind it a bit. Of course he could not understand why Thumper laughed so hard when another animal popped up out of the flowers, and Bambi called him, "Flower!" It really was funny though, because you see, Flower was a skunk. And skunks are not the sweetest smelling of animals, especially not when they get excited. Oh my, most certainly not when they get excited.

One morning, Bambi's mother took him to a wonderful place. It was called 'the meadow'. What a nice place that was for a young fawn to romp around and have fun. It was there that Bambi met Faline.

Faline was very cute to be sure. At first Bambi was a little afraid of her, well, maybe not so much afraid as he was shy. But soon they were racing around and having a grand time chasing one another. When all of a sudden, there was a horrible, loud noise, like thunder! All the animals were running very swiftly. They were being led by 'The Prince of the Forest'. He was very old, and very strong. But he was also very, very wise. He knew he had to lead all the animals in the forest to safety. The one word that would do that was 'MAN'. Oh yes, all the animals knew that word. They knew it meant there was danger close by. So they did not waste any time, they ran as fast as they could. When it was safe, they all returned to their homes, and Bambi lay comfortably, safe and protected by his mother.

Winter soon came to the forest. At first Bambi had lots of fun. Thumper tried teaching him to slide on the ice. As Bambi learned, Thumper just watched and laughed till he was rolling on his tummy. Poor Bambi, his four thin legs just went every which way, and down he would go again. Even though it was fun, it was also a hard time for Bambi and all the other animals, because the cold had rid the ground of its soft green, tender carpet of grass, and sweet tasting flowers. There was little to eat, except tree bark.

'BAM' there it was again. The same deafening sound Bambi had heard before. His mother yelled for him to run for the thicket. "Quick," she yelled. Bambi reached the thicket. But...but where was his mother. She had been right behind him, and now... she was not there.

Once again, Bambi saw the 'Great Prince Of The Forest'. "Your mother can no longer be with you. You must learn to walk alone," he said to Bambi in a stern but somber voice. What was the Great Prince telling him? Did he mean Bambi would never see his mother again? Yes, he knew that was what the Great Prince was saying. Bambi was alone.

At last winter left, and spring returned. Everything was

green again. Bambi had grown much bigger. He was no longer a fawn, now he was a "Buck". A buck is a male deer, much older than a fawn. As the spring went on to summer, Bambi roamed the forest and the meadow until one day he met Faline again. She had grown into a very beautiful graceful doe. Yes, that is what a grown up girl deer is called, a 'doe'. Just as they were beginning to enjoy being friends again, another buck came charging between them. He did not want Feline to stay with Bambi. He wanted Feline to stay with him. A terrible fight began. They kept charging at each other, bumping their foreheads against the other real hard. Finally, the mean old bully was hurt and limped off all alone. Bambi and Feline walked off into the forest together.

As spring and summer had gone, autumn arrived in the forest. The trees took on a breathtaking array of colours. And the air had a very special crispness to it. But sadly, all this beauty did not last. One day, Bambi began to smell something. And as he ran to find Feline, The Great Prince came. He told them to run very quickly, for the forest was on fire. Feline raced for protection, as Bambi and the Great Prince ran to warn all the other animals. At last, the fire was over. Bambi, Feline, and the Great Prince looked on at the terrible thing that the fire had done. All the colours were gone. There was a terrible smell of burned wood and blackened trees. A fire is a terrible thing, it destroys everything it touches. As they stood there, gazing at what remained of the smoldering forest, it was then that the Great Prince told Bambi, that when the forest was green again, he would be very old, and Bambi would have to take his place.

At last Spring arrived again. Green leaves, green grass, and wild flowers began to cover up some of the damage the fire had done. And now do you know what was happening. All the animals were running to see. Not one new fawn, but two of them. They were cuddled next to their mother, Feline. And where was Bambi, why he was high on a hillside, looking down. His chest was puffed out, and he was standing there as proud as he could be. For not only was he a new father, but now Bambi was the new Prince of the Forest.

The Four Wives

There was a rich merchant who had four wives. He loved the fourth wife the most and adorned her with rich robes and treated her to delicacies. He took great care of her and gave her nothing but the best.

He also loved the third wife very much. He's very proud of her and always wanted to show off her to his friends. However, the merchant was always in great fear that she might run away with some other man.

He loved his second wife as well. She was a very considerate person, always patient and in fact was the merchant's confidante. Whenever the merchant faced some problems, he always turned to his second wife and she would always help him out and tide him through difficult times.

Now, the merchant's first wife was a very loyal partner and had made great contributions in maintaining his wealth and business as well as taking care of the household. However, the merchant did not love the first wife and although she loved him deeply, he hardly took notice of her.

One day, the merchant fell ill. Before long, he knew that he was going to die soon. He thought of his luxurious life and told himself, "Now I have four wives with me. But when I die, I'll be alone. How lonely I'll be!"

Thus, he asked the fourth wife, "I loved you most, endowed you with the finest clothing and showered great care over you. Now that I'm dying, will you follow me and keep me company?"

"No way!" replied the fourth wife and she walked away without another word.

The answer cut like a sharp knife right into the merchant's heart. The sad merchant then asked the third wife, "I have loved you so much for all my life. Now that I'm dying, will you follow me and keep me company?"

"No!" replied the third wife. "Life is so good over here! I'm going to remarry when you die!" The merchant's heart sank and turned cold.

He then asked the second wife, "I always turned to you for help and you've always helped me out. Now I need your help again. When I die, will you follow me and keep me company?"

"I'm sorry, I can't help you out this time!" replied the second wife. "At the very most, I can only send you to your grave." The answer came like a bolt of thunder and the merchant was devastated.

Then a voice called out, "I'll leave with you. I'll follow you no matter where you go." The merchant looked up and there was his first wife. She was so skinny, almost like she suffered from malnutrition. Greatly grieved, the merchant said, "I should have taken much better care of you while I could have!"

Actually, we all have 4 wives in our lives

(a) The fourth wife is our body. No matter how much time and effort we lavish in making it look good, it'll leave us when we die.

(b) Our third wife is our possessions, status and wealth. When we die, they all go to others.

(c) The second wife is our family and friends. No matter how close they had been there for us when we're alive, the furthest they can stay by us is up to the grave.

(d) The first wife is in fact our soul, often neglected in our pursuit of material, wealth and sensual pleasure.

A Box full of Kisses

It was Christmas time and so everyone in the family was decorating gifts to give them to their loved ones. Suddenly something caught daddy's eyes and he punished his 3-year-old daughter for wasting a roll of gold wrapping paper. Money was tight and he became infuriated when the girl tried to decorate a box to put under the Christmas tree. Nevertheless, the little girl brought the gift to her father the next morning and said, "This is for you, Daddy."

The man was embarrassed by his earlier overreaction, but his anger flared again when he found out the box was empty. He yelled at her, stating, "Don't you know, when you give someone a present, there is supposed to be something inside?"

The little girl looked up at him with tears in her eyes and cried, "Oh, Daddy, it's not empty at all. I blew kisses into the box. They're all for you, Daddy."

The father was crushed. He put his arms around his little girl, and he begged for her forgiveness.

Only a short time later, an accident took the life of the child. It is also told that her father kept that gold box by his bed for many years and, whenever he was discouraged, he would take out an imaginary kiss and remember the love of the child who had put it there.

In a very real sense, each one of us, as humans beings, have been given a gold container filled with unconditional love and kisses... from our children, family members, friends, and God. There is simply no other possession, anyone could hold, more precious than this.

Two Frogs

A group of frogs were traveling through the woods, and two of them fell into a deep pit. When the other frogs saw how deep the pit was, they told the two frogs that they were as good as dead.

The two frogs ignored the comments and tried to jump up out of the pit with all their might. The other frogs kept telling them to stop, that they were as good as dead. Finally, one of the frogs took heed to what the other frogs were saying and gave up. He fell down and died.

The other frog continued to jump as hard as he could. Once again, the crowd of frogs yelled at him to stop the pain and just die. He jumped even harder and finally made it out. When he got out, the other frogs said, "Did you not hear us?" The frog explained to them that he was deaf. He thought they were encouraging him the entire time.

This story teaches two lessons:

1. There is power of life and death in the tongue. An encouraging word to someone who is down can lift them up and help them make it through the day.

2. A destructive word to someone who is down can be what it takes to kill them.

Be careful of what you say. Speak life to those who cross your path. The power of words... it is sometimes hard to understand that an encouraging word can go such a long way. Anyone can speak words that tend to rob another of the spirit to continue in difficult times. Special is the individual who will take the time to encourage another.

■■■

Other Books on

WORD POWER SERIES

1. Effective English Comprehension Read Fast, Understand Better ! **(New)**
2. Latest Essays for College & Competitive Examinations **(New)**
3. Dictionary of New Words **(New)**
4. Art of English Conversation Speak English Fluently **(New)**
5. Teach Yourself English Grammar & Composition **(New)**
6. Common & Uncommon Proverbs **(New)**
7. Effective Editing Help Yourself in Becoming a Good Editor **(New)**
8. Effective English A Boon for Learners **(New)**
9. Essays for Primary Classes
10. Essays for Junior Classes
11. Essays for Senior Classes
12. Dictionary of Synonyms and Antonyms
13. Dictionary of Idioms and Phrases
14. Common Phrases
15. How to Write & Speak Correct English
16. Meaningful Quotes
17. Punctuation Book
18. Top School Essays
19. How to Write Business Letters with CD
20. Everyday Grammar
21. Everyday Conversation
22. Letters for All Occasions
23. School Essays & Letters for Juniors
24. Common Mistakes in English
25. The Power of Writing
26. Learn English in 21 Lessons
27. First English Dictionary
28. Boost Your Spelling Power
29. Self-Help to English Conversation
30. The Art of Effective Communication
31. A Book of Proverbs & Quotations
32. Word Power Made Easy
33. English Grammar Easier Way
34. General English for Competitive Examinations
35. Spoken English
36. School Essays, Letters Writing and Phrases
37. How to Write & Speak Better English
38. Quote Unquote (A Handbook of Famous Quotations)
39. Improve Your Vocabulary
40. Common Errors in English
41. The Art of Effective Letter Writing
42. Synonyms & Antonyms
43. Idioms
44. Business Letters